国家出版基金项目
江苏省"十四五"重点图书出版规划项目
侵华日军南京大屠杀遇难同胞纪念馆资助项目

波兰
华沙

WAR-SAW

Poland

International Cities of Peace

Series Editor: Liu Cheng
Associate Editors: Ling Xi   Chen Junfeng

Marcin Tomasz Damek

NANJING NORMAL UNIVERSITY PRESS 1995
南京师范大学出版社

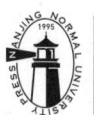

United Nations Educational, Scientific and Cultural Organization
UNESCO Chair on Peace Studies
Nanjing University
People's Republic of China

图书在版编目（CIP）数据

波兰·华沙 = Warsaw, Poland：英文 /（波）达昕（Marcin Tomasz Damek）著. -- 南京：南京师范大学出版社，2022.8
（国际和平城市丛书 / 刘成主编）
ISBN 978-7-5651-5407-2

Ⅰ.①波… Ⅱ.①达… Ⅲ.①华沙—概况—英文 Ⅳ.①K951.35

中国版本图书馆CIP数据核字(2022)第133854号

丛 书 名	国际和平城市丛书
丛书主编	刘　成
丛书副主编	凌　曦　陈俊峰
书　　名	Warsaw, Poland
学术顾问	［波］卡齐米日·乌齐斯基（Kazimierz Wóycicki）
著　者	［波］达昕（Marcin Tomasz Damek）
策划编辑	徐　蕾　郑海燕
责任编辑	刘双双
书籍设计	瀚清堂
出版发行	南京师范大学出版社
地　　址	江苏省南京市玄武区后宰门西村9号（邮编：210016）
电　　话	(025)83598712（编辑部）83598919（总编办）83598412（营销部）
网　　址	http://press.njnu.edu.cn
电子信箱	nspzbb@njnu.edu.cn
照　　排	南京私书坊文化传播有限公司
印　　刷	上海雅昌艺术印刷有限公司
开　　本	889毫米×1194毫米　1/32
印　　张	8
版　　次	2022年8月第1版　2022年8月第1次印刷
书　　号	ISBN 978-7-5651-5407-2
定　　价	50.00元
出 版 人	张志刚

* 南京师大版图书若有印装问题请与销售商调换
* 版权所有　侵犯必究

Foreword by Series Editor

This book series, International Cities of Peace, Volume I, introduces five cities, which have one thing in common that they have all experienced the trauma of war in their history, and the collective memories have endured from one generation to the next. So, history must be kept in mind. Only by looking back on past sufferings and using history as a mirror can we prevent such historical tragedies from occurring again. It is absolutely vital to recognize and remember the historical trauma, but how we remember it may affect its authenticity and how long we will keep it in mind. According to history, building peace is the best remedy for remembering and recovering from the past suffering. When the traumatic memory of a city is transformed into a common human memory, we can understand the past disasters in a new way beyond stereotyped political memory. Only this can enable the traumatic history to be linked to the future peace, which can promote the reconciliation between the former hostile parties, and boost hope to the establishment of a community with a shared future for mankind. History indicates that reconciliation means not only exchanging our views and experiences of the past, but also a process of mutually creating new ideas for the future and sharing new experiences. In this way, reconciliation is a thought and a power that meets our mutual needs, which can be developed by building cities of peace with the legacy bequeathed by the war. That is why we wrote these books.

All the five cities of the book series are actively engaged in building a culture of peace. Nanjing, the first International City of Peace in China, held an international peace forum on positive peace; Dresden reflects on the war experience of Germany and strengthens domestic and international reconciliation; Hiroshima leads non-governmentally the anti-nuclear peace movement in Japan; Warsaw promotes the reconciliation dialogue that has led to a shared historical memory both inside and outside Poland; Coventry is the benchmark for British reconciliation. At the same time, the study of war memory is undergoing changes in three dimensions: shifts from the hero memory to the traumatic memory, from the memory of a victorious country to the memory of all the wounded countries, and from the domestic historical memory of a country to historical memory shared by many countries. Our belief is that the memory of war will be ultimately eclipsed by the memory of peace, as more and more cities work towards building cities of peace and thus form a global network of peace cities.

The five cities have their own characteristics in building a city of peace. Their practice of building peace has proven the truth that "There is no way to peace; peace is the way". Cities of peace all share a common purpose, promoting the culture of peace advocated by UNESCO, that is, working to build peace through conflict prevention, mediation and transformation; providing peace education on non-violence, tolerance, acceptance, respect and sustainable development; promoting intercultural dialogue and reconciliation. To build a city of peace requires the joint efforts of governments, universities, social groups, non-government organizations and citizens from all countries and regions around the world, for it needs to incorporate elements of peace in historical records, memories and heritage. It can be achieved in many ways, such as conflict prevention, peace-keeping, peace-building, peace research, peace education, and all peace activities that promote urban progress and prosperity as well as world peace and development.

This book series rests on its disciplinary foundation, Peace Studies. With the only UNESCO Chair on Peace Studies in China, Nanjing University is widely recognized as the center of China's Peace Studies. The development of China's Peace Studies has received great help from many institutions and individuals around the world. Without their support, Peace Studies would not have developed in China, and these books would not have been published, either. This book series took ten years to compile, experiencing ups and downs along the way, and finally came out. All the authors, translators and editors have done their best to bring out these books against all the odds, and make them authentic, scholarly, innovative, and readable at the same time.

This book series is an attempt to understand how cultural trauma and historical memory affect us. We sincerely welcome readers to point out and correct the defects and mistakes in these books.

Liu Cheng
Professor, School of History, Nanjing University
Chairholder of UNESCO Chair on Peace Studies
August 2022

Contents

001

Foreword by Series Editor

006

Introduction

008

Chapter 1 **History: Past Experiences of Warsaw**

Becoming the Capital of the Commonwealth	012
National Capital without Its State	030
Warsaw during the Interwar Period	042
Warsaw during World War II	056

072

Chapter 2 **Memory: Remembering the War at the Time of Peace**

How to Remember Warsaw's Past	076
Rebuilding the Capital and Building the Narrative	088
A Stabilized Narrative	106
The Narrative Shift during the Time of Changes	126
The Resurgence of the Past	140

Chapter 3 Peace and Reconciliation Process: Warsaw Peacebuilding and the Polish-German Dialogue

Concepts of Peace, Studies of Peace and Reconciliation — 162

Between the "Fighting for Peace" and the Reckoning with the Past — 167

The Breakthrough in Peace and Reconciliation — 176

Reflecting on the Past for Peace — 191

Peace and Reconciliation at the Time of Transformation — 210

Cherishing Peace and Reconciliation despite the Challenges — 236

Main Bibliography

Afterword

Introduction

Go to Warsaw city center and the first thing you notice is the ubiquitous presence of monuments. They bear testimony to the city's history, its most important events from the past. Similarly, understanding a city's history is essential for fully comprehending its landscape. Once we grasp what happened and what is remembered, we can build solid foundations for peace and reconciliation.

I graduated from the University of Warsaw and spent more than five years in this city. After graduation, I was enrolled in the Ph.D. candidate program in Chinese History offered by Nanjing University. From the start, I noticed that both cities share many similarities. Both cities suffered heavy losses during the war. After the war, stories of both cities sparked a national debate on how to commemorate the past and how to get along with former enemies.

The main body of the book is divided into three parts. In Chapter One, we are going to outline Warsaw's complicated past. By providing an overview of the history, discussing the most important sites and buildings, and making a sketch of life in the city, we may fully comprehend what kind of Warsaw was inevitably lost. To put it simply, what happened in Warsaw? Chapter Two deals with memory changes and narrative building, that is, how the city's war experience was remembered and commemorated. I tried to catch the multidimensional nature of the narrative building process. You, dear reader, might be puzzled by all the different actors during different stages of time, all of them wanting to add their opinions to the city's main story. What was to be remembered, by whom and how?

When talking about the traumatic experience, remembering the past is a tool to reconcile with the past, with oneself, and with the other: including the former perpetrator. Part three focuses on post-war peace and reconciliation. What was the role of Warsaw in the Polish-German dialogue? Not only did the city's experience limit to being a part of broader national reconciliation, Warsaw's past also gave an impulse for peace activism and peace culture. If that was the case, what term should we propose to fully convey the Warsaw experience as a Peace City?

I am going to end this introduction here by asking a question of this synthesis. But before we attempt to answer it, we need to start with another introduction: this time to the complicated and turbulent history of Warsaw.

Chapter 1

History: Past Experiences of Warsaw

As a city that experienced wars, internal conflicts, and reconstructions, Warsaw's past experiences were unique. Moreover, not only did these past events shape the future of the Polish capital but also played a pivotal role in the country's history as a whole. To understand the collective memory and peacebuilding process of such a place as Warsaw, it is crucial to grasp the city's history—as well as to understand it within the larger scope of the Polish national narrative.

Becoming the Capital of the Commonwealth

City's name Warsaw or *Warszawa* in Polish is many times explained through the legend about a couple of fishermen Wars and Sawa who were founders of the city. In other accounts, the city's legendary founding is attributed to the help of a mythical guardian who decided to protect the future settlement. Originally, this guardian was depicted as a creature with a male human body and animal elements (bat wings, duck feet, and reptile tail). Later on, it evolved into a half-fish half-human mermaid, that is, into what we know as the contemporary Warsaw symbol [Fig.1-1].

Fig.1-1 One of the earliest depictions of Warsaw. A depiction of the Warsaw Emblem (center) could be seen next to Latinized name for the city: "Varsovia."

When there is a legend, there is the actual history. First permanent settlements in the area of what is now known as Warsaw appeared in the 9th century. From the 10th century onwards, local rulers of these areas built successive strongholds (grody). Each stronghold protected potential urban development. The fact that these structures (stronghold plus surrounding dwellings) were located near the Vistula River provided a steady economic incentive for growth. However, this area together with the broader region of Masovia suffered from raids conducted by northern and eastern neighbors. Warsaw lands faced pillaging conducted by the Lithuanian armies from 1262 to 1263. Such raids convinced local feudal lords to build up military defenses. Structures became firm enough to stabilize Warsaw's situation, so much that it was granted township rights. As Andrzej Zahorski noted, "the most probable hypothesis is that this allocation of (township rights) took place around 1300". From that point onwards, we may describe Warsaw as a city.

Until the year 1526, Warsaw was ruled by the dukes of Masovia. After their line came to the end, the city became a part of the Polish royal domain. Andrzej Zahorski stressed that even Warsaw was still a middle-sized city within the Kingdom of Poland. Despite that, Warsaw was already "on its way to becoming the capital". The city's increasing importance coincided with major changes that arrived with the 16th century and the Polish Renaissance. During this period, the Kingdom of Poland and its neighbor, the Grand Duchy of Lithuania, was ruled by the same monarch coming from the Jagiellonian dynasty. In 1569, two countries formed a union state known as the Polish-Lithuanian Commonwealth. Having approximately 1 million square kilometers, the Commonwealth comprised lands of contemporary Poland, Lithuania, Latvia, Estonia, Belarus, Ukraine, and Russia. From the 16th to the 18th century, it was one of the largest countries in Europe. As a consequence of owning different lands, the Commonwealth was home to people from different religions and ethnicities.

The country implemented a system that often is referred to as the "noble democracy". After the death of Sigismund Augustus II in 1572, who was the last ruler of the Jagiellonian dynasty, the monarch of the Polish-Lithuanian Commonwealth became an elected office. The noblemen of the Commonwealth were allowed to partake in the elections where candidates could come from the domestic and foreign aristocracy. The newly elected king had the right to rule the entire country till his death and the new elections, but this came under certain conditions. Every new monarch was obliged to guarantee noblemen's rights. These included: the right for noblemen to elect the king, the obligation for the king to make decisions under the approval of the noblemen's parliament (called the Sejm [Fig.1-2]), and the necessity for the king to respect religious tolerance within the country. Within the system, the noblemen secured their dominant political role, controlling not just the king, but also other classes: peasantry, city dwellers, and clergymen. They called the country Rzeczpospolita, coming from the Latin term Res publica, the Republic. As historian Adam Zamoyski noted: "There was an obvious paradox in the co-existence of monarchy and republic, yet the Poles made a virtue out of the seeming contradiction."

Fig.1-2 Sejm proceedings during the reign of Sigismund II Augustus. Every Polish-Lithuanian Sejm had three main entities partaking in the proceedings: the king, senators, and deputies.

Fig.1-3 Warsaw Confederation original manuscript. The UNESCO "Memory of the World" program states that the document "introduced peaceful co-existence for nobles of all denominations".

Warsaw became one of the most important cities within the Polish-Lithuanian state—also in terms of national politics. In 1569, the very same Sejm in Lublin which decided on the formation of the Commonwealth also made another important decision. Warsaw became a main location for the Polish-Lithuanian Sejm. On 28 January 1573, the parliament ratified the so-called Warsaw Confederation—a document that confirmed religious tolerance within the Commonwealth [Fig.1-3]. A few months later, the nobles gathered in Warsaw to choose a new king during the first royal election.

In 1596, King Sigismund III from the Vaasa dynasty moved the royal court from Cracov to Warsaw. The decision to move the capital to Warsaw was connected with general politics during that era. Throughout his life, king Sigismund III wanted to restore his right to the Swedish throne which he had lost as a result of a power struggle. Apart from that, Sigismund's reign also coincided with a period of Russian history that is often known today as the "Time of Troubles". In 1598, the Russian Tsar Fyodor I died without a clear successor to the throne. The succession crisis resulted in political turmoil in Russia which, in turn, evolved into a military conflict. King Sigismund wanted to use this situation for his plans: to convert Russia to Catholicism and install the Vaasa dynasty on the Russian throne. After the Battle of Klushino in 1610, the Polish-Lithuanian Army started occupying Moscow. One year later, the Commonwealth commander Stefan Żółkiewski presented to the king the deposed Russian Tsar Vasili Shuisky [Fig.1-4]. The initial success in campaign did not last long. The Russian forces led by Dmitry Pozharsky and Kuzma Minin expelled the Polish

Fig.1-4 Tribute made by the deposed Russian Tsar Vasili Shuisky to the Polish King Sigismund in Royal Castle of Warsaw.

garrison from Moscow in 1612. The War slowly came to the conclusion. In 1613, the Russian noblemen called boyars chose Mihail Romanov to become the next Tsar. The Truce of Deulino of 1619 and the Polanów Treaty of 1634 effectively ended the hostilities.

It is not the role of this book to analyze deeply 17th century politics. But, we may see that in these turbulent times, Warsaw became a convenient seat for the king to coordinate politics of the Commonwealth towards Sweden as well as Russia. As Andrzej Zahorski noted, the reign of King Sigismund III "was long, and for Warsaw, it was a very important one". Even though Kraków remained the place of royal coronations, it was Warsaw that became the political center of the country. King Sigismund and later monarchs resided in the Royal Castle in Warsaw. The city also became a permanent place of proceedings for the Sejm. Last, but not least, Warsaw fields were the site of royal elections. By combining these three elements, Warsaw became the *de facto* capital of the Commonwealth. In 1644, a column honoring King Sigismund was erected next to the Royal castle.

Sigismund III was an ambitious monarch. However, he and his successors were not always successful in wars against powerful neighbors. Apart from Russia, the Commonwealth had to fight long wars with other great powers, including Sweden and the Ottoman Empire. During these wars, Warsaw experienced occupation and many of the city's areas were destroyed. Warsaw suffered greatly during Polish-Swedish War which happened between 1655 and 1660. "Between 1655 and 1657, Warsaw witnessed enemy forces several times awaiting on her walls." Andrzej Zahorski also noted that the main street of Warsaw called Krakowskie Przedmieście (the Cracov Suburb) along with areas of Nowe Miasto (New Town) were ruined. "Nearby villages were burnt down too." Due to war and epidemic, Warsaw's population fell from 18,000 in 1655 to 6,000 in 1659. After the war ended in 1660, Warsaw entered a period of considerable development. Polish monarchs such as Jan III Sobieski's powerful noblemen families (e.g. Krasiński family) funded the construction of palaces, churches, and other buildings in Baroque architecture. This period effectively came to an end with destructions caused by the Northern War (1700-1721).

Despite these damages, the 18th century was marked with overall development for Warsaw. The Commonwealth at the time was ruled by two consecutively elected kings from the same Saxon dynasty: Augustus II and Augustus III. Augustus II and his architects put forward the so-called Baroque Axis (also known as the Saxon Axis)—one of the very first plans for urban development of Warsaw. It centered around a future royal residence called the Saxon Palace. The palace was to be integrated with the Royal Castle, residences built by the noblemen and Warsaw city in general. The plan was continued during the reign of King Augustus III. The cosmopolitan nature of the city made it an attractive place for foreign immigrants. Merchants, architects, artists, and other people from Saxony, Italian principalities, France and Scotland immigrated to Warsaw. As Andrzej Zahorski noted: Some foreigners arrived in Warsaw from Saxony which was ruled by the same monarch. Others looked for new opportunities or evaded religious persecution back home.

The urban planning and construction of new buildings, cosmopolitan atmosphere (bolstered by the presence of foreigners) slowly changed Warsaw into an Enlightenment Era metropolis. Developments in education were also visible. Originally, catholic orders such as the Jesuits and Piarists championed enhancing Warsaw literacy. Printing houses were set, journals such as 1729 *Kurier Polski* (The Polish Messenger) and periodicals were printed. New education institutions, which specifically targeted educating noblemen, were established within the city. Such examples included Collegium Nobillum which was founded in 1748. These developments were continued during the reign of the next king Stanisław August Poniatowski (also known as Stanislaus II Augustus) who was elected in 1764 [Fig.1-5].

Fig.1-5 Royal Elections of 1764 chose Stanisław August Poniatowski as the final king of the Commonwealth. The visible in the painting election field was located in present-day Warsaw.

With the reign of the new king, the above-mentioned education and culture developments continued and the city witnessed these changes. King Stanisław supported establishing higher education institutions. These included the so-called Szkoła Rycerska (Corps of Cadets) which was founded in 1765. Such schools eventually became a backbone for the future establishment of the University of Warsaw in 1815 (long after the partition of the Commonwealth and the king's abdication). King Stanisław also took patronage new trends in architecture: Warsaw Royal Castle was renovated, a new route called Droga Królewska (Royal Alley) was proposed as an urban design. The period also marked the development of classical architecture. Artists were hired by the monarch and the city culture flourished. Those changes in the city landscape were later depicted by Bernardo Bellotto [Fig.1-6], one of the king's court painters.

Fig.1-6 Warsaw in the 18th century. The painting depicts a view on the Cracow Suburb (Krakowskie Przedmieście), one of the city's main streets. King Sigismund's Column as well as part of the Royal Castle are visible to the left.

The last king Stanisław August attempted to modernize the country with the help of enlightened nobles and under the protectorate of the Russian Empire. However, neither Russia nor two other powerful neighbors of the Commonwealth—Prussia, and Austria, were interested in such attempts. All three powers started to interfere in local political affairs. In 1772, three countries agreed on the first partition of Poland-Lithuania. One year later, the decision was signed during the Sejm procceding in Warsaw. After the first partition of Poland, the Sejm gathered in 1773 to confirm the decision of the Commonwealth's neighbors. The decision triggered the Commonwealth reform-minded politicians to seek change.

In the advent of the French Revolution, Warsaw was the place of the 4-year Grand Sejm discussions, starting from 1788. The parliament proceedings eventually resulted in the enactment of Constitution of 3rd May 1791 [Fig.1-7].

These reform attempts were soon to be stopped by the intervention of foreign powers. In 1792, Russia organized loyal noble forces and declared war on the new constitutional monarchy. Seeing no chances for success, the king eventually sided with the Russian Empire against the reformists. The War lasted one year and resulted in the second partition of 1793. In 1794, Polish nobles allied with peasants under the command of Tadeusz Kościuszko organized an insurrection. The insurrection—sometimes referred to as the first national uprising—succumbed to overwhelming Russian forces. Warsaw once again saw damage during the conflict. In 1795, Russia, Prussia, and Austria made the final third partition. Poland disappeared from European maps for 123 years [Fig.1-8].

Fig.1-7 Constitution of 3rd May 1791. The nobles together with the king are celebrating the passing of the constitution in front of the Royal Castle.

Fig.1-8 The Fall of Poland—Polish Painter Jan Matejko's artistic interpretation of the year 1773, during which the Sejm accepted the First Partition. Series of partitions eventually led to the disappearance of the Polish. Lithuanian Commonwealth.

National Capital without Its State

After 1795, Warsaw and nearby territories became a part of the Prussian Kingdom. The situation, however, did not last for too long. The European continent saw the rise of the French Revolution: for many Polish politicians and officers, French revolutionary wars, and subsequent Napoleonic Wars could be a chance for restoring Polish independence. In 1797, the "Polish Legion" was formed in Milan: it assisted the French Army in fights against the Austrian Empire. After Napoleon's accession to power and his successful campaigns against Austria, Prussia, and Russia, a new Duchy of Warsaw was formed under the conditions of the Tilsit Treaty of 1807. It became a protectorate of the French Empire. By 1812, approximately 90,000 Polish soldiers had joined the Grand French Army in its campaign against the Russian Empire. However, the attempt was unsuccessful for Napoleon. In 1815, the period called Napoleonic wars came to an end. The Vienna Congress organized by European Great Powers shaped the post-war order.

Based on Vienna Congress proceedings, Warsaw became part of the newly-formed Kingdom of Poland and its capital. The "Congress Poland" (as it was formed after the Vienna Congress) possessed a constitution that guaranteed independent parliament, administration, and judiciary. The Kingdom also had its autonomous army. Thus, in theory, the newly-established kingdom was an autonomous region within the Russian Empire, where the Russian Tsar was simultaneously the Polish King. He and the central imperial administration in Petersburg decided over external affairs and controlled Polish matters by an institution of viceroys (pol. namiestnik, rus. наместник). However, such an arrangement proved to be vulnerable against different expectations of involved parties. The liberal-minded Polish noblemen and young political activists treated it as a chance for restoring Polish independence. Meanwhile, the Russian imperial administration demanded loyalty to the state and Russian conservatives accused the Poles of being "ungrateful" to the Tsar. Consequently, the autonomy of the region was gradually suppressed which only lead to further escalation of the conflict.

These tensions eventually resulted in the November Uprising (1830-1831), an attempt of achieving Polish independence by military action. The outbreak of insurgency took place in Warsaw. During the night of 29th-30th November, conspiring officers captured the city's arsenal [Fig.1-9]. They attempted abducting grand duke Konstantin who was at the time the main commander of the Polish Army. Initially, the Polish Sejm and moderate politicians attempted negotiating with the Tsar and controlling the mutiny in the army. However, the Tsar demanded an unconditional surrender. On 25th January 1831, the Polish

Fig.1-9 The capture of the arsenal in Warsaw depicted by Marcin Zaleski. The event marked the beginning of the November Uprising (1830-1831).

parliament dethroned the Tsar. These events eventually led to a bloody conflict between the Russian army and loyal tsarists on one side, and the insurgent Polish army on another. Warsaw became the battlefield during the last days of the conflict which ended with Tsarist Russia's victory. Tsar Nicholas I abolished the constitution of Congress Poland which effectively ended the autonomy of the region. The University of Warsaw and other educational institutions throughout the former Commonwealth were closed. The Tsar ordered the construction of the Warsaw Citadel: a military garrison which was to play its role in future events.

Despite the failure of the November Uprising, further limitations of regional autonomy only led to another rise of a political conspiracy against the Russian Empire. The conspiracy culminated in the January Uprising: an armed insurgency which lasted from 1863 to 1865 [Fig.1-10]. Unlike its November predecessor, the January Uprising was an example of guerilla warfare. The insurgents dispersed their forces throughout the country in small detachments. Consequently, the suppression of the insurgency proved to be challenging for the Russian forces with the last insurgents being defeated in the spring of 1865.

Fig.1-10 The Branka (Conscription) of 1863. As a counter-measurement against a potential armed insurgency, the Russian Army ordered a conscription of Polish males in Congress Poland. Contrary to expectations, the decision provoked Polish independence advocates to launch a full scale national uprising.

Originally, Warsaw was to become the center of the Temporary National Government, but the insurgents failed to capture the city. Thus the Polish authorities needed to act in secrecy. The city possessed a strong military garrison of Russian forces. One of its components, the already mentioned Warsaw Citadel – became the place of executions of political figures supporting the Uprising side. That was the place where the last military dictator of the Uprising Romuald Traugutt was hanged in 1864. His death in Warsaw Citadel marked one of the final episodes of the January Uprising.

After the January Uprising, the political autonomy of what was referred to as Congress Poland or as "Vistula Land" was limited to the status of another province. Limitations included the replacement of the Polish language in favor of Russian. The source of this policy, though grounded in distrust of Russian central authorities after the uprising, could be also grounded in a broader context. In his work *Imagined Communities*, Benedict Anderson described the crisis of absolutist monarchy whose legitimacy was originally based on non-national ideas. By contrast, during the 19th century, especially during its second half, the justification of monarchs' rule was increasingly based on ethnic criteria. Anderson noted that the Romanovs "discovered they were great Russians". Here, the common language was increasingly seen as an important force: Not only did it create a link between rulers and subjects, but it could also unite people within the empire. This reasoning was opposed by other ethnic elites, including the Polish patriots.

Warsaw could be a good example of how such policies worked in practice. Adam Zamoyski noted that the city's university was reopened in 1862 as the Warsaw Main School (Szkoła Główna Warszawska). By 1869, the School was replaced by the Imperial University of Warsaw with Russian as the main language: usage of Polish was in turn restricted. "In 1885 Russian was substituted for Polish as the teaching language, even in elementary schools. Children were not allowed to address each other in anything but Russian within the precincts of the school." In a response to such attempts, Polish patriotic circles would promote secret education curriculums.

Fig.1-11 The Great Synagogue in Warsaw. During the 19th century, the Jewish community comprised a large percentage of Warsaw city dwellers.

Apart from politics, the 19th century marked many social-demographic changes in Polish lands. The noblemen gradually transformed into new social strata called the intelligentsia. Rapid industrialization led to the disappearance of traditional craftsmanship and the emergence of the working class. Apart from purely economic division, the society at the time was also ethnically diverse. In the lands of Congress Poland/Vistula Land, the Poles lived together with Russian immigrants as well as the Jewish community. Warsaw was at the center of these changes. In 1816, 81,000 people were living in Warsaw; among them, 15,000 were Jewish. In 1830, the number grew to 126,000 for the entire city and 30,000 Jews, respectively. By 1897, Warsaw possessed a population of around 700,000 people; among them more than 35% were Jewish [Fig.1-11].

Apart from social-demographic changes, the 19th century also brought development for Warsaw architecture. Architects in the first half of the century focused on neoclassical architecture. One of the best examples of this tendency was the Grand Theater [Fig.1-12]. The Theater together with other buildings was grouped around a single space: The Theater Square. Later buildings in the second half of the 19th century were built in newer styles: neo-gothic, neo-renaissance, and secessionist ones. Warsaw was gradually transforming from an Enlightenment Era city to 19th century modern metropolis.

During this development, some areas of Warsaw retained their former characters: the Warsaw Old Town Market Square is one such example [Fig.1-13]. At the same time, new areas and districts flourished in Warsaw, some having their unique character too. Between the area of Ujazdów and the Old Town, there was a coastal district called Powiśle. Located at the bank of the Vistula River, Powiśle became an industrial region of Warsaw, where fishermen, craftsmen, and (later on) factory workers lived together. Other regions of Warsaw also expanded: Wola and Ochota to the West, Praga district to the East.

Fig.1-12 Warsaw Theater Square with the Grand Theater. Built between 1826 and 1833, the Theater became a significant place for Polish high culture.

Fig.1-13 The Warsaw Old Town Market Square. The photograph was taken around the year 1900.

Along with socio-cultural changes came the economic and technological ones. The city saw changes in the landscape. Railroads were built: the first lane linking Warsaw with the Austrian-controlled Galicia Region was completed in 1846. Modern sanitation was brought to the city: major changes came in between 1880s and 1900s. Warsaw inhabitants received access to cleaner water, street gutters were gradually replaced with the sewage system. Gas installations provided heat to residential buildings. Thanks to these improvements, the city's hygiene level greatly improved and inhabitants' mortality rates lowered. New facilities did not end here. Tramway lanes (horse-run initially, later electric ones) were introduced and expanded in the city. In 1856, the first steel bridge in the city was built [Fig.1-14]. By the turn of the century, Warsaw entered a new epoch as a modern metropolis, the 3rd largest in the Russian Empire.

Fig.1-14 Warsaw around 1900. Kieberdź Bridge is visible in the front, in the back Warsaw Royal Castle together with the Old Town.

The new situation emerged with the advent of the World War I. In 1914 Germany and Austria-Hungary engaged in military operations against the Russian Empire. In 1915, the German Army entered Warsaw and started occupying the city until the end of the war. Meanwhile, the Poles living in different empires were soon to be mobilized to fight against one another. During the War, there were whole formations comprised only of Polish people. One of such formations, the so-called Polish Legions (Legiony Polskie), was formed in 1914. Led by Józef Piłsudski, the Legions were aligned with the Austria-Hungarian Empire.

Such developments did not go unnoticed by Germany, Russia, and Austria-Hungary—all sides wishing they could mobilize the Poles in their war endeavors. In order to win minds of the Polish people, all former partitioners had to address in one way or another the question of Polish independence. On 5th November 1916, a declaration of German and Austria-Hungarian emperors was announced. It promised that post World War I Poland was going to be an autonomous entity allied with the two monarchies. Based on promises of the declaration, German authorities formed in 1917 the Regency Council of the Kingdom of Poland—a new body which was officially responsible for governing Polish lands. As Adam Zamoyski noted, the Germans still needed Józef Piłsudski's support for their undertakings in swaying Polish public opinion to their side as well as convincing the Poles to fight for central powers. Piłsudski, however, refused to cooperate and in July 1917 was put under arrest. Despite that, it was Piłsudski who eventually emerged as a prominent political figure in these changing times.

In 1917, the Russian Tsar abdicated after the February Revolution. The Russian Provisional Government was formed; the Empire of Russia became the Russian Republic. However, the government led by minister-president Alexandr Kerensky was overthrown a few months later during the October Revolution. Power in Russia was seized by the Bolshevik revolutionaries. Led by Vladimir Lenin, the Bolsheviks decided to end the war with Central Powers. The Brest Treaty signed in March 1918 ended Russia's engagement in World War I.

After the Brest Treaty, the Central Powers continued their engagements with the Entente forces. Initially, the German Army launched a successful attack on the Western front. Not long after, the offensive stopped. With the arrival of the US army in the West, the Germans could not continue their advancement and found themselves to be the defensive side soon after. Ultimately, the Central Powers were overwhelmed by the Entente on all fronts. On 11th November 1918, an armistice between Germany and combined French-UK representatives was signed in Compiegne. The armistice together along with armistices signed with the rest of the Central Powers put effectively the conflict to an end. The World War I was over.

As German Empire was to be replaced by the Weimar Republic, as Austria-Hungary was dissolving into several countries and as Russia plunged into a civil war, circumstances finally started to favor Polish independence. On 7th November 1918, Polish Transitional Government was formed by Ignacy Daszyński. On 10th November 1918, Józef Piłsudski returned from the German incarceration to Warsaw. One day later, on 11th November 1918, he was conferred all powers by the Regency Council. As Adam Zamoyski noted, Piłsudski declared publicly in Warsaw that "the Polish state has arisen from the will of the whole nation".

Warsaw during the Interwar Period

A newly reborn Poland had to fight for the preservation of its independence from the very beginning. To the West, Polish Borders were mostly settled as a result of several factors combined. The first factor was the armed insurrections. Uprisings in regions of Greater Poland (1918-1919) and Silesia (1919-1921) played roles in incorporating these areas into Polish State. The second factor was regional referendums. After the war, people in the disputed regions were asked about their statehood identity and incorporated into the state they voted for the most. The third final factor was decisions conducted by the victorious Entente coalition. Under the Treaty of Versailles (1919) and minor agreements, foreign powers of the United Kingdom, France, and the United States determined the shape of future countries: mostly at the expense of former Central Powers such as Germany. The central government in Warsaw observed these developments. For Warsaw as a city, perhaps what turned out to be more important were developments in the East.

After the collapse of the Russian Empire, the political void was filled by various factions which competed against one another. The Bolsheviks had to face new enemies in their quest of securing power. The list of anniversaries included national movements of the collapsing Russian Empire, the White Army which aimed at restoring the monarchy and which was supported by the foreign powers, the anarchists, and other minor groups. To the East, the Poles were already in combat with the Ukrainian armies regarding future borders. During the first months of the year 1919, the Polish Armed Forces saw minor skirmish battles with the Bolshevik Red Army. Piłsudski, who at the time was the main political figure in Poland and the most important military commander, decided that Poland should not engage further in the conflict. The Bolsheviks canceled Partition Treaties signed by the Russian Empire and at least guaranteed temporal stability of Eastern Polish borders. On the other hand, the White Movement saw restitution of the Russian Empire with its borders before World War I. For the Whites, no acceptance of Polish independence was possible.

However, once the Bolshevik Red Army had an upper hand in their fight with the White Movement, skirmishes between Soviet Russia and Poland gradually evolved into a full-scale war. In May 1920, Polish troops reached Kyiv, but soon the Red Army started its offensive. In August 1920, the Bolsheviks reached the outskirts of Warsaw preparing for the final assault against Polish forces. To the Red Army commanders' surprise, the Poles launched a successful counteroffensive [Fig.1-15]. During the Battle of Warsaw, the Bolsheviks were forced to retreat. Fightings continued till the armistice of 1921, but overall, the Battle of Warsaw proved to be the decisive turn of the war. The new Polish Republic survived. It would be commonly known as the Second Republic, a term which indicated Poland having a tradition of a republican form of governance. It implied that the

Fig.1-15 The Battle of Warsaw of 1920. The defense of Poland's capital became a turning point for the Polish-Soviet War of 1919-1921.

post-1918 Polish state was perceived as a successor to the Polish-Lithuanian Commonwealth: the original noblemen republic. Warsaw once again became the country's capital, this time both *de iure* and *de facto*.

During the War and after it, Polish politicians took efforts to construct a coherent political system for the state. In February 1919, provisional Sejm was formed. For the time of war, most of the political power was put on shoulders of Józef Piłsudski, but it was the newly created Polish parliament that was to formulate the national constitution. The law was ratified in March 1921, thus later called "the March Constitution". Poland's political system was modeled after the French Third Republic. The Parliament consisted of the lower house called the Sejm and the Upper House which was referred to as the Senate (Senat). The president was to be elected by the Sejm every 7 years. Within this system, the function of the Polish head of state was predominantly representative. The Sejm secured its dominant position and became the most decisive political body within the new Republic.

What was perhaps envisioned as a counter-measurement against the autocracy became a problem for the Polish state. The Sejm, whose members were elected through a general election, was for most of its time fractured between different political parties. Major factions included socialists, conservative national-democrats, the peasant-based agrarian movement participants, the representatives of different ethnic minorities. The political divisions did not limit themselves only to parliamentary debate. When President Gabriel Narutowicz was elected in 1922, he soon became a victim of these clashes. Being supported by socialists, the agrarian movement participants, and the minorities, he was assassinated by a national-democrat supporter.

Later on, power struggles followed one after another, making the political situation very unstable. As Adam Zamoyski noted, the situation provoked an increasing desire for "strong government". In May 1926, Józef Piłsudski and military officers loyal to him decided to launch a coup d'Etat. Piłsudski supporters captured Polish Parliament Seat and Presidential Palace in Warsaw. The May Coup proved to be a turning point. The parliamentary democracy was gradually replaced by a new form of governance. The main element of it was the *sanacja*, a political movement that advocated for the sanation/healing of the country. It favored establishing stronger authoritarian rule with Piłsudski as its central figure. After he died in 1935, politicians of *sanacja* continued to rule Poland until World War II.

Warsaw was the site of these political developments, but one observed social changes in the country as well. In 1921, the population living within the Polish state was estimated to be about 27 million. By 1939, there were roughly 35 million citizens in the Republic of Poland. Among them, two-thirds of inhabitants were farmers; one-third of the population represented various occupations: factory workers, craftsmen, merchants up to wealthy elite. Interwar Poland was a multiethnic society too: about 65% of people were ethnic Polish. One-third of its citizens were representatives of ethnic minorities, including Jews, Ukrainians, Belarussians, Germans, Tatars, and others. Then, some divisions echoed former partitions. As Adam Zamoyski noted: "Along with four legal systems, the Republic inherited six different currencies, three railway networks, and three administrative and fiscal systems."

The city was to become a unifying force for the country despite itself being highly diverse and divided. The population of a city rose from around 750,000 in 1918 to over 1 million in 1935, reaching almost 1.3 million inhabitants in 1939. Warsaw inhabitants were very diverse: politically, economically, and ethnically. In terms of economic division, Warsaw's local elites just accounted for 2 percent of the total population. These included government high-rank officials, industry businessmen, house estate holders, and landed aristocracy. The next group was petite bourgeoisie which made up 20% of the population: shop owners, craftsmen, merchants, street vendors, and others. Another 20% represented intelligentsia and white-collar workers. The majority of inhabitants belonged to a broadly defined proletarian working class: their share in the Warsaw population varied from 40% to 50%. Here, the peculiar sub-class was the so-called lumpenproletariat—people living in chronic poverty and unemployment for a long time. Due to its situation, some of its members would resolve themselves into theft, robbery, and other crime-related activities.

Apart from economic disparities, Warsaw also possessed an ethnic diversity: with a very strong Jewish community at its core. In 1938, it was comprised of over 300,000 people. As Marian Marek Drozdowski noted, the majority of Jews lived in the so-called "Northern District" and the northern part of Śródmieście district [Fig.1-16]. Muranów, Powązki, Leszno, Grzybów, and parts of the Old Town region: all were areas in which Warsaw Jews were dominant ethnicity. In terms of their material status and occupation, some aspects distinguished the community from the ethnic Polish majority. The Jews were active in trade-related occupations; they also excelled as white-collar workers of the private sector: mostly as doctors, lawyers, and private school teachers. Statistically, more Jews belonged to the

Fig.1-16 Nowolipki Street in Warsaw during the interwar period. Warsaw Jews lived in a distinct Jewish Quarter. Nowolipki was one of its main streets.

petite bourgeoisie than their ethnic Polish counterparts. The Warsaw Jewish community also possessed the most populous Jewish urban proletariat in Poland and entire Europe: its number exceeded 100,000.

It is not surprising then that the Jewish community had its distinct political, social and cultural life. The left-wing political parties such as the Bund engaged in hot debates with right-wing orthodox and Zionist associations such as Agudat over the future of the community. Over 100 primary schools, several kindergartens, and vocational schools provided education for the Warsaw Jews. Hospitals, orphanages, and shelters for the poor provided social security. Jewish press and Jewish theaters were stimulating intellectual life. Many of the above-mentioned endeavors were supported by the Board of the Jewish Community (Zarząd Gminy), a local representation of Warsaw Jews.

Since we mentioned the issue of governance within the Jewish community, it is worth noting what the administration of the city looked like at the time. From the end of World War I until 1934, Warsaw was primarily governed by the City Council (Rada Miejska). However, tensions between the *sanacja*-oriented central government and the City Council resulted in change. Starting from 1934, a commissionary rule controlled by the central government decided upon municipal matters. Its main figure was president Stefan Starzyński [Fig.1-17]. Being the politician of the *sanacja* movement, Starzyński and his supporters issued many plans to renew the city, to make it a formidable, European metropolis. Plans included stabilizing the municipal budget, enhancing construction and investments, raising the aesthetic beauty of the city, and renewing the city's infrastructure.

Fig.1-17 Stefan Starzyński in 1934. Starzyński was the final mayor of Warsaw before World War II.

The city landscape changed as well. Some buildings which were constructed during the time of the Russian Empire were dismantled after the reclamation of independence in 1918. It was mostly due to the public perception of some buildings with Russification [Fig.1-18]. On the other hand, there were many undertakings of restoring old palaces and monuments. Warsaw Royal Castle and the Grand Theater were renovated.

New developments were also visible in Warsaw. In Żoliborz, new housing estates for military officers, government officials, and members of the intelligentsia were constructed. Some of them were built in the new mansion-like style which imitated residences of former noblemen. Elsewhere, the modernist type flourished: its architects emphasized simplicity, functionality, and new solutions in designed buildings. The city center at Śródmieście experimented with monumental architecture: Main Railway Station being one example of this tendency.

All in all, the interwar Warsaw was a thriving metropolis, one of the most populous cities in Europe. It was also a city with many contrasts: a world of wealthy elites and intelligentsia at Żoliborz, the Jewish community of the Northern District, the place of the working class of Warsaw living in Powiśle and Praga.

As Marian Marek Drozdowski concluded describing inter war Warsaw:

> *Warsaw during the interwar period— a city of high social and economic mobility, a place which concentrated on basic political and economic decisions, which shaped political views, cultural-artistic and moral norms—played an important role in integrating Polish territory divided by the partitioners. Warsaw played this role by inspiring new economic ties, overcoming the economic impact of the partitions, and inspiring psychological-cultural ties, which broke district separatisms. As the largest metropolis of the Second Republic, Warsaw did serve its function as the national capital, not only formally but also in reality.*

One might see the character of Warsaw City Center by looking at pictures taken before 1939 [Fig.1-19]. We can imagine what Warsaw lost after the War. Perhaps it is important to remember this portrait of a city as it would resurface later—when it would become a memory because of the incoming war.

Fig.1-18 Warsaw in 1919. The Alexander Nevsky Cathedral (visible at the main square next to Saski Palace), was removed after World War I.

Fig.1-19 Jerusalem Alleys in Warsaw during the interwar period. The picture was taken in 1934—1935 years before World War II.

Warsaw during World War II

On 1st September 1939, Nazi Germany invaded Poland. Originally, the Poles expected the war to be a short one. Prior to the conflict, the Polish government formed an alliance with the United Kingdom and France against possible aggression of Nazi Germany. The Allies, however, decided not to partake in any major military operations. In addition, the German forces were backed by the Soviet Union. In accordance with the Hitler-Stalin Pact, the Soviet Red Army attacked Poland on 17th September 1939. This led to the situation where the Polish Armed Forces had to face two enemies, both having superior armies in terms of equipment and strategic position. According to Adam Zamoyski, the German Army alone possessed a formidable force of 1.5 million soldiers, 2,700 tanks, 1,400 warplanes. By comparison, the Polish side had 1 million soldiers, 600 tanks, and 400 warplanes. Despite the disparity, the Republic of Poland Armed Forces continued its defiance.

Warsaw was bombarded during the very first days of the War [Fig.1-20] and starting from 13th September, the city found itself under siege. Despite the odds, the Warsaw garrison continued fighting and was aided by the civilian administration under president Starzyński. The defenders of the Polish capital finally succumbed to German forces on 27th September 1939. Later on, the last Polish forces surrendered on 5th October 1939. The Polish Government in Exile was formed: originally set up in Paris, it was moved to London following the French defeat in 1940.

Fig.1-20 Royal Castle damaged during an airstrike on 17th September 1939. Throughout the September Campaign, Warsaw experienced heavy bombardment from the German Luftwaffe.

Back in Poland, Polish territories occupied by Nazi Germany were split into two parts: one became incorporated directly into the German Reich, the remaining parts became known as the General Government with its capital in Kraków. Even though it remained the largest city within the German-occupied area, Warsaw symbolically lost its capital status, which was a deliberate choice by the German occupants.

Soon after, the new administration started to implement racial policies in accordance with the Nazi ideology. The Germans were to be considered a master race. Slavic peoples, the Poles being their most notable group, were classified as races inferior to Germans. They were deprived of the right for higher education, entertainment and everyday facilities such as transportation were restricted. According to Nazi politicians, the Poles as well as other Slavs should be reduced in favor of future German colonists. The remaining Slavic people should become the cheap labor force serving the superior race.

The worst treatment was to be reserved for the Jewish people. Since the beginning, the Jews were restricted to newly formed Warsaw Ghetto. They were not allowed to leave the area without special permission. To allow better identification, they were forced to use special armbands: the so-called "King David Star" on a white background. Food ratios were severely limited and access to culture and everyday facilities restricted. The wall [Fig.1-21] was built around the Ghetto to separate the Jewish Ghetto from the rest of the city. All the Jews in Warsaw had to live in the Ghetto. Anyone leaving the Ghetto without a special permit was treated with death penalty.

Harsh policies imposed by the occupants resulted in defiance. After the defeat of 1939, the Polish Underground State was formed to organize the resistance movement. The beginnings were modest ones: one of the earliest actions included what was later remembered as the "small sabotage". Groups of resistance members, many times juveniles, would choose visible city sites to write slogans and make drawings which would mock the occupants and discourage people from any collaboration. Notable symbols included the "PW" sign, the acronym of the term "Polska Walcząca"—the fighting Poland. Combining two letters "P" and "W" would form a sign which would be also referred as "the anchor". The sign would be adopted by the Home Army (Armia Krajowa in Polish, or the AK for short), the most prominent fighting force within the resistance movement. Its predeceasing organizations were formed in 1939 and 1940, later to be transformed into the AK in 1942. According to Adam Zamoyski, it was the biggest resistance force in the occupied Europe, roughly comprising 300,000 members at its peak. Its goal was to prepare both Warsaw and other occupied territories for the national uprising. Other goals of the resistance included the aid for the Jewish people.

On the Jewish side, things turned more dramatic in 1942. The Nazi politicians' debates upon the final solution, that is, how to resolve the Jewish question, reached its zenith. During the conference at Am Wannsee, the plan was approved to launch full extermination, usually by means of existing concentration camps and with the establishment of the death camps. For Warsaw, this meant that all the Jews living inside the Ghetto were to be transferred to concentration and death camps. Inside the Ghetto, people were informed that they were going to be relocated to new labor camps.

Fig 1-21 The construction of Warsaw Ghetto walls. The Warsaw Ghetto was constructed after the German army secured its dominance in occupied Poland.

The real intention behind "the relocation" were known to the resistance within and outside the Ghetto. The remaining Jewish population—mostly young men able to bear the burden of labor work—formed paramilitary organizations within the Ghetto. When the German army entered the area on 19th April 1943 to disband the Ghetto, to their surprise, they were met with fierce defense. This was the start of the Warsaw Ghetto Uprising. Despite being outnumbered by the German Armed Forces, the insurgents' defiance lasted till 16th May 1943. The surviving Jewish people were to be put in the Warsaw Concentration Camp organized within the former Ghetto, some of them managed to be rescued by the resistance movement. The Ghetto itself was turned into ruins [Fig.1-22].

Fig.1-22 Destroyed Warsaw Ghetto. The suppression of the 1943 Uprising cemented the fate of Jewish Quarters.

Despite the defeat, the year 1943 turned out to be decisive for the resistance movement. On the Eastern Front, the Nazi Germany war machine suffered defeats in the battles of Stalingrad and Kursk. Meanwhile, the Western Allies repelled Axis forces in North Africa. By mid 1943, combined British and American forces landed in Sicily. The Allies continued their advance in continental Italy. By June 4th 1944, they managed to liberate Rome. On 6th June 1944, the Allies opened another front by landing in Normandy—a northern region in France. After several weeks of combat, French capital Paris was liberated. On all of these fronts, the Poles marched side by side with Allied forces. The German Reich was put under heavy pressure on all fronts.

The Polish Underground State and the Home Army leaders realized that the Soviet Red Army was going to enter territories of Republic of Poland. This resistance was mostly loyal to the London-based Government in Exile (often referred to as "the London Government"). Meanwhile, the Soviets backed Polish forces organized in the USSR, furthermore, pro-Soviet political bodies were established by politicians of Polish Workers Party (PWP, or Polska Partia Robotnicza, the PPR). In such a situation, the Home Army prepared for launching an insurgency in Warsaw as well as for partisan actions targeted at liberating Polish lands—before the Red Army could arrive. Both sides were thinking ahead: future liberators were to decide about the post-war order in Poland.

As the Soviets were moving closer to Vistula River's right bank, the Home Army leaders decided to launch the Uprising. On August 1st, 1944, the insurgents attacked German forces in Warsaw and managed to secure a substantial part of the city. The Uprising was backed not just by the Home Army, but also by other resistance forces as well as the civilians. Flags of the occupants were removed: for the moment, there was an overwhelming enthusiasm for the insurgency [Fig.1-23].

Fig.1-23 War reporter Stanisław Bala "Giza" removing German flag during the "W" hour—an official start for the Warsaw Uprising.

Fig.1-24 Wola district Massacre. The Warsaw Uprising also affected the lives of civilians: people who were not engaged in direct combat. There, around 60,000 civilians were killed by the German SS.

After initial gains by the insurgents, the Wehrmacht retook tactical initiative. Within the first days after the outbreak of the Uprising, the German Army captured the Wola district, perpetrating a massacre of local people [Fig.1-24]. From August till mid-September, the insurgents were, in general, losing their ground against enemy forces in all districts. Some people guessed that the Uprising was going to end sooner than later.

As the insurgents continued their combat, they received the news about the arrival of the Red Army. Located on the right bank of the Vistula River, a city's district called Praga was secured by the Soviets in September. The Polish 1st Army, which was fighting together with Soviet Forces, was about to set a perimeter on the left side of Warsaw. On 16th September, its infantry division landed on the other shore of the Vistula River. Yet the unit was poorly trained and failed to coordinate its actions with the insurgents. After a week of intense combat, the division returned to the Red Army-controlled right bank of the Vistula River.

The insurgents continued fighting for another two weeks. Throughout the conflict, the insurgents compensated for their weaknesses by the determination of their soldiers. Many of them were adolescents [Fig.1-25]. Shortages in arms were managed by them by seizing equipment from the enemy, including pistols, machine guns, up to armored vehicles. Despite these undertakings, the insurgents were increasingly overwhelmed by casualties (both military and civilian); no prospects of victory could be seen either.

As a result of these two factors, leaders of the resistance decided to cease military actions. On 2nd October 1944, the Home Army high command signed an act of surrender to the German side.

The Warsaw Uprising ended after 63 days. In total, around 15,000 insurgents were killed. On the German side, there were from 2,000 up to 17,000 casualties. In addition, the fights resulted in the death of about 150,000 - 200,000 civilians. Overall, the total death toll of the Uprising is estimated at roughly about 200,000 people. Soon after the Uprising ended, the remaining civilians and insurgents (now recognized as Official Allied Forces) were to be sent to labor camps and leave the city [Fig.1-26]. Very few people who decided to stay in Warsaw were surrounded by vast ruins and hastily prepared mass graves.

Fig.1-25 Young insurgents from "Radosław Regiment", 2nd September 1944. Many of the insurgents were adolescents, aged 14-18 years old.

Fig.1-26 Refugees from the Warsaw Uprising. The Warsaw Uprising was also a tragedy for civilians, people who were not engaged in direct combat.

The Uprising meant not only the loss of human lives but also further damages of the city landscape. Due to the intensive combat, many of the widely recognized Warsaw buildings were torn down. A photo taken during the Uprising depicted the Prudential Building being damaged by the artillery barrage. By the time it was one of the tallest skyscrapers in the city. The war was not merciful to more traditional architecture either: the Old Town and the Royal Castle were all in ruins [Fig.1-27]. In addition to combat-caused destruction, the Nazis planned to annihilate the city from the beginning of the war. The period after the Uprising was perceived as the right time since it would be interpreted as a punishment to the Polish people.

When the Red Army and Polish forces fighting alongside it finally crossed the Vistula River in January 1945, its soldiers entered a completely different city than it used to be before the War [Fig.1-28]. The city which originally had 1.3 million people before the War became largely abandoned: only about 3,000 people were hiding in Warsaw ruins in January 1945. Most people were killed during uprisings, killed in concentration and death camps, or sent to labor camps. The annihilation of Warsaw's population was followed by the destruction of the city's architecture.

World War II in Europe ended on the 8th of May 1945. This meant a new beginning for both Poland and Warsaw.

Fig.1-27 Destroyed Old Town. The Warsaw Uprising and actions conducted by the German occupants resulted in the ultimate destruction of the city.

Fig.1-28 Polish soldiers standing in front of ruins. On January 17th 1945, the Polish 1st Army Troops entered destroyed Warsaw.

Chapter 2

Memory: Remembering the War at the Time of Peace

During World War II, Poland lost approximately 6 million people. Apart from human casualties, the country suffered material losses too. Many Polish cities and villages were utterly destroyed, Warsaw being a notable example. The city, which had boasted of a population of 1.3 million, lost most of its city dwellers. But not only did the buildings have to be rebuilt, the past waited to be remembered.

How to Remember Warsaw's Past

When facing the past, we may ask two very different questions. The first one, concerning the actual past, is more of the domain of traditional historiography. Here, we can recall the words of Prussian historian Leopold von Ranke who was one of the most prominent historians in the 19th century. According to him, history wanted only to show "how it essentially was" (wie es eigentlich gewesen). Traditionally, historians focused on political history, military history, and the history of diplomacy. By quoting documents and other sources, historians wished they could reconstruct an objective view of the past. In other words, the main concern for this kind of research is to answer the following question: "What happened?"

But that is just one aspect, another one is more concerning not the objective reality, but rather one's experience of the past. This brings us to the category of collective memory. The idea was coined and promoted by French sociologist Maurice Halbwachs in such works as "The Social Framework of Memory" (*Les Cadres Sociaux De La Mémoire*) and "The Collective Memory" (*La Mémoire Collective*). The core idea is that societies can have a collective memory which has its framework. The framework exceeds the limitations of one individual, it is shared by many people at the same time. By comparison to more traditional historiography, the research which is about the collective memory and the narrative about it focuses more on the following questions: How do people remember? How do people tell stories of the past?

Several terms can help us understand the chapter. As Marcin Król noticed in his analysis of Maurice Halbwachs, the French sociologist distinguished between collective memory and history memory (or simply history). "Collective memory is a continuous flow of thoughts; this continuity is completely natural; everything from the past will initially be preserved, but gradually those memories that are no longer alive in the consciousness of the group will be lost." By contrast, "history is not interested in continuity, it pays attention to changes and differences and not to similarities, it is outside any group viewpoint and it classifies events from this external standpoint". The second difference is that history is one and unified whereas "there are as many collective memories as there are social groups". Last but not least, history does not look at past events through the prism of the present. On the other hand, the collective memory cannot be detached from the present.

Halbwachs theory was later developed by Jan and Aleida Assmann. Jan Assmann distinguished two types of memory: communicative one and cultural one. Sylwia Dec-Pustelnik in her monograph summarized Jan Assmann's communicative memory as the one which "includes memories of the immediate future, and its typical variety is generational memory". Kazimierz Woycicki elaborated on this topic in his book *Niemiecka Pamięć* (German Memory). In a chapter regarding Historiography of Memory, he noted that for Assmann, memory is a social process, in which the image of memory evolves and constantly changes. Communicative memory "seems to be in this process in a sense first and primary". However, once witnesses of a certain event pass away, the communicative memory disappears—what emerges instead is the cultural memory. During such a transition, as Sylwia Dec-Pustelnik noted, "remembering the past will be moved to the outer realm", a move from oral accounts of witnesses to written records and broadly understood public space. An individual experience of the past, which we can describe as communicative memory, becomes a part and is contextualized in broader cultural/collective memory.

But how? Here, two additional categories can be useful for understanding the problem of remembering. Firstly, apart from a conversation, memory can be passed through a medium. Sylwia Dec-Pustelnik summarized Aleida Assmann's notions of what can be memory mediums. A medium can be something written (in a form of a book) as it "records everything what can be put into words". It can be visual or spatial too, for the latter category, Assmann listed statues and cemeteries as possible memory mediums. Secondly, some mediums do stand out because of their spatial capabilities and their potential ranges. These are called sites of memory—a term frequently used by French historian Pierre Nora. Kazimierz Wóycicki notes that "if one wishes establishing the connection between two terms", we could say that "a site of memory is a kind of medium of the past, whose recalling of the past is read in the same way"—thus universally understood. Site of memory "possesses clear and symbolic character" and could be described as a "central to peculiar community medium of memory".

Both sites of memory and memory mediums are not chosen by historians. "Popularity of symbol or and icon is a combination of many elements, including mass media, decision, and construction of museums. It could also be linked with whether or not the symbol is ready to be accepted by the general public." It is not surprising that sites and mediums become important during the transfer from communicative memory to cultural memory. Even at the time when witnesses of the event are still alive, the memory is ritualized through national holidays, statues, museums, and other means/sites of memory. Even though witnesses disappear, the memory—now a cultural one—persists.

Memory in general, no matter whether it is communicative memory of a group or cultural memory of the whole society, differs from history. History itself can be said to be a study of the past. However, history work does not register the past, but as such—it is a form of a narrative. Kazimierz Wóycicki noted that "Work of a historian, similar to that of a fiction writer, has its plot". And, if we proceed one step further, the same applies not to just the writing of a particular historian, but the overall existing narrative within a particular society. In other words, any society has its own story about what happened—and this narrative is widely accepted.

This phenomenon is often defined as the fundamental narrative. German scholar Trutz von Trotha, who was quoted by Kazimierz Wóycicki, defined elementary narrative as a "history construct of a particular society or particular culture which contains dominant legitimization for constructing the past. Thus changes within the elementary story always foretell fundamental changes to one's society political culture". It is to say that the fundamental narrative arranges one's society or culture into a coherent vision of the past. Moreover, such a narrative is mostly a result of mixing many existing narratives within a society. To be broadly understood, the fundamental narrative is organized by commonly understood historic symbols.

Kazimierz Wóycicki concluded that "by cataloging memory containers, describing emerging sites of memory, observing evolutions of each narrative, analyzing how the image of the past is staged, not only is a historian able to see how the recent past looked like, but also how it was remembered—even though a historian would never know how the past is going to be written in cultural memory". For peace researchers, such a method is valuable. Peacebuilding, reconciliation, and dialogue happen by addressing memory about the past and not just the past as it happened. After providing a theoretical framework, let us discuss further what these terms mean in practice.

First, we may consider people who witnessed the past. Every person tends to remember certain events while simultaneously forgetting about other ones. Moreover, as time passes by, the memory of that witness is affected: one tends to forget about the details of a particular experience. Naturally, one memory can be remembered by different people at the same time. If they are in contact with each other, they may tell together their own experiences, thus building a broader picture, up to the point it reaches the entire society's collective memory. Here, the communicative memory is present—experiences of particular individuals are told to and shared with others. Another aspect is that many times one person may tell the story to the next generation, thus memories about past experiences could survive and exist in the future. Yet here, communicative memory slowly becomes a cultural one. The next generation cannot listen to living witnesses anymore, but it can utilize all memory mediums available.

Naturally, the transition process may alter the memory. Former generations may consciously and unconsciously alter the story they tell to the young. A possible example of that could concern memories about violence, when one side was a victim, whereas the other was a perpetrator. Former victims are going to retell the story of their victimhood. In the case of perpetrators, some of them may tell their act as it was done, yet others would deliberately or not deliberately diminish the crime they had committed.

The situation is getting more complicated when we consider the problem of building the narrative about the past. As it was said, one can tell his memories to the others, thus starting the storytelling process. But one also writes down his memories. In the writing process, one's memory is going to be arranged—some elements of the past will be written down, whereas other things will be omitted. But what if the author is not the witness of the past, but a professional historian instead? Supposing that some historians have the Leopold von Ranke paradigm in their mind, they will try to reconstruct the past as it was.

However, once the basis of the research is found in other people's memories, then the question emerges concerning historians' objectivism. Despite one's good efforts, a historian cannot avoid the subjectivity of memory influencing the writing process.

Another note could be added when building a historical narrative serves political purposes. Where there is society, there is someone who governs it. Benedict Anderson, when describing the concept of an imagined community, discussed how people can believe that they belong to a group bounded by a common territory, culture, and history. Enforcing such a belief is often linked with the actions of a state. Eric Hobsbawm and cooperating scholars noticed a phenomenon of a so-called invented tradition. Traditions many times do not have a long history of themselves; rather, they pretend that they were always there. The book *Invention of Tradition* gave an example of it by using Scottish clan tartans—even though the idea of the tartan comes from the 19th century, the tradition towards the kilt make the society believe that the concept is much older and can be traced together with origins of Scottish nation—the imagined and shared community.

Political leaders are aware of phenomena regarding the past and memory. National governments use practices of cultivating memory to rally the society under one cause. The practice of cultivating memory does not belong to governments as such. People may tell their stories, write down their memoirs or visit particular places to pay tribute to the past. The difference is that the government adds a political aim towards the political memory. The government is going to support the narrative which matches its political interests and deny (even suppress) alternative narratives. Such clashes and fusions eventually lead to solidifying the fundamental narrative—one which can determine societal and cultural understanding of the past.

Various sites, such as buildings, natural objects, or more structured ones, including museums, monuments and plaques, all of which help to cultivate shared identity. The political power may favor one site of memory over another, paying more emphasis on cultivating it. Moreover, it can affect the meaning of a particular site, for instance by renaming a street from one patron to another, by erasing old monuments and erecting new ones, even by slightly changing inscriptions on plaques. These all count as the process of historical narrative building.

When these developments happen in a particular state, then the function of its capital is an important one. By its status, national capital makes its own experiences a subject of national history, at the same time, it serves as a microcosm of national memory. That is to say, on one hand, experiences of the capital are discussed within the national narrative (through history textbooks, national events, etc.), at the same time, the capital many times places memorials in its landscape which are not necessarily connected with capital's history as such. A good example of it are monuments and graveyards. Before the War, Warsaw had two important cemeteries: Old Powązki Cemetery and Powązki Military Cemetery. The Old Powązki Cemetery was established in the late 18th century and became a place of burials of Polish nobles, intellectuals, and those who contributed to the development of Polish society [Fig.2-1].

On the other hand, the Military Powązki Cemetery was constructed before World War I and—as the name suggests—was mainly for those who fought in combat. That included veterans of national uprisings and armed conflicts: January Uprising (1863-1864), World War I (1914-1918), the Greater Poland Uprising (1918-1919), and the Polish Bolshevik War (1919-1922) just to mention. The Military Powązki Cemetery shows that identity-related to war and national risings was important for the Polish nation [Fig.2-2]. Both Old Powązki Cemetery and Military Powązki Cemetery also show what was discussed in the previous chapter, that the history of Warsaw was linked very firmly with national history. Many events central to the past of the Polish nation happened in the country's capital.

Before we start discussing the post-war narrative building, we need to add a few remarks which will make later processes to be discussed more understandable. Generation of Warsaw inhabitants who witnessed the War entered the post-war era with their memories and experiences. Some of these could be traced back to generations that preceded them.

Fig.2-1 Old Powązki Cemetery. Established in the 18th century, the cemetery also became the place of memory for the Warsaw insurgents.

Fig.2-2 Powązki Military Cemetery. Veterans who were engaged in a particular conflict have separate quarters. This photo depicts quarters dedicated to World War I soldiers.

The first aspect which should be noted is the emergence of a negative source of identity. The entire 19th century was a history of emerging modern Polish nation without having its national state. Therefore, identity was constructed not solely on the foundations of who we are, but also on who we are not. Examples of such tendency could be seen in many ways of expressing group identity, including religion. During the nation-building process, Catholic Christianity became increasingly associated with Polish, also because it was not a denomination of those held by Poland's partitioners. The Germans (especially northern ones) were Protestants, whereas the Russians were Orthodox: attempts to spread these denominations at the time of partitions were met with defiance by Polish patriots. Such dichotomies appeared in other identity expressions, let it be language ("we" speak Polish, "they" speak Russian or German) or war ("we" fought together against "them"). Such rhetoric of bringing Poles together against "the other" was also a problem for post-war narrative building and as we show later, for the post-war peace and reconciliation process.

The second aspect would be the importance of the noblehood strata, which later evolved into intelligentsia. The nobles launched the November Uprising of 1830-1831 and the January Uprising of 1863-1864, which were to be later considered national ones. After two risings failed, the representatives of intelligentsia devoted themselves to extending national consciousness to other classes of society. After World War I, despite the official abolishment of noble titles, the intelligentsia still influenced national politics. After World War II, the intelligentsia retained a great influence over the Polish identity, which also included influencing the narrative of history. Many postwar government officials or public intellectuals came from the intelligentsia strata. In a way, we could argue that post-war narrative building which determined future peace and reconciliation in Warsaw was linked with social hierarchy and very influential individuals.

Last, but not least, what was important for Poland and Warsaw as such was their relationship with the Jewish heritage. The Jewish community which settled during the Middle Ages flourished in the Renaissance and the Enlightenment period, whose integrity became an important topic in the 19th century and which was almost annihilated during World War II, had to influence the post-war historical narrative building. Warsaw Jews and Polish Jews, in general, suffered greatly during the War. The question remained how their heritage and wartime tragedy was to be remembered and narrated after the War ended.

Rebuilding the Capital and Building the Narrative

As we mentioned earlier, politicians gathered around the Polish Workers Party (Polska Partia Robotnicza, PPR) and the Polish Government in Exile (also known as the London Government) did not cooperate during and after the War. Instead, the PPR formed its governmental structures—Temporary Government of National Unity (Tymczasowy Rząd Jedności Narodowej, TRJN), which some of the non-communist forces decided to join. Backed by the Soviet Union, the PPR gradually marginalized other groups: in 1948, it merged with remnants of the Polish Socialist Party (Polska Partia Socjalistyczna, the PPS) to form a new political force—Polish United Workers Party (Polska Zjednoczona Partia Robotnicza, the PZPR). The PZPR became the dominant political force for the next 40 years. In 1952, parliament passed the new constitution which settled the new name for the country—Polish People's Republic (Polska Rzeczpospolita Ludowa, the PRL).

Such were the beginnings in post-war Poland and Warsaw, a period of history that started in 1945 and ended in 1989. That being said, these times were not simply a product of domestic developments. Even if we look at the first sub-stage within Polish People's Republic, the period of the late 1940s and early 1950s will be remembered as years of Stalinism. Polish political system at that time resembled the one which was established in the USSR under Joseph Stalin. It was also at the time the dominant political order of the Eastern Bloc, a group of Central-Eastern European Countries sharing the same ideology and being in one political alliance strengthened in organizations such as Communist Information Bureau a.k.a. Cominform (since 1947 till 1956), Council for Mutual Economic Assistance a.k.a. Comecon (since 1949) and the Warsaw Pact (since 1955).

Within this new reality, older and newer generations were facing the dilemmas of the past. Members of the oldest generations remembered times before Poland's independence. Younger ones tended to be connected more with the interwar period (1918-1939). As a result, experiences of the war varied as well—some were at the time military commanders whereas some witnessed wartimes as young soldiers or civilians. There were also individuals who at the time were too young to remember the War themselves, but who experienced the post-war order (people born in the late 1930s onwards).

Immediately after the war, the first question emerged—what to do with destroyed Warsaw? In the beginning, there were suggestions put forward by some politicians to move the capital elsewhere, for instance to the nearby city of Łódź. However, many Warsaw inhabitants returned to the city after the War. Despite most of the dwellings being ruined, many of them decided to continue living in Warsaw, some started repairing their houses on their own. It occurred to new rulers of postwar Poland that rebuilding the city could be treated as a new source of legitimacy to rule the country. Furthermore, the Polish Workers Party leaders held January 1945 meeting with Soviet leader Joseph Stalin. During the meeting, Stalin informed the PPR representatives that Warsaw should be rebuilt and that such an undertaking was going to be backed by Soviet assistance. Thus it was decided not to abandon Warsaw.

Fig.2-3 A popular slogan "The entire nation is rebuilding its capital" engraved on a tenement house in the vicinity of Nowy Świat/Marszałkowska intersection in Warsaw.

In February 1945, the Capital Reconstruction Bureau (Biuro Odbudowy Stolicy) was founded. It aimed to coordinate Warsaw rebuilding under the new political order. People of Warsaw joined reconstruction undertakings, they were soon to be supported by funds and nationwide and immigrant workers from other regions of Poland. To describe such a phenomenon, the slogan "The entire nation is rebuilding its capital" (Cały naród buduje swoją stolicę, see [Fig.2-3]) was widely used in national propaganda. It helped to popularize an image, according to which, Poland's capital rose from the ashes. But the slogan also indicated another interesting phenomenon that occurred in postwar Poland. As the national capital, Warsaw was rebuilt, but it did not simply mean constructing new buildings and reconstructing those which perished in World War II. Warsaw was symbolically rebuilt as a site of memory—through the efforts of the people of Warsaw, Polish citizens, and the state as a whole.

Some places, such as the Old Town, were reconstructed from scratches. Some places were abandoned and demolished. They were replaced in favor of new buildings for the city; filling the landscape with new symbols took place as well. We may perceive the Palace of Culture and Science as being a part of such an endeavor [Fig.2-4]. Built between 1952 and 1956, the palace was envisioned as a piece of the new socialist realist architecture, a multi-functional building where museums, theaters, cinemas, educational institutions could be organized. What also mattered was the symbolic meaning behind the Palace. Designed by Soviet architect Lev Rudniew, the palace was presented as a contribution of the USSR in rebuilding Warsaw. Both Polish and Soviet workers were involved in the construction of the Palace. Last but not least, the final project for the building strongly resembled skyscrapers built in Moscow which are collectively known as "Stalin's high rises" or "Seven sisters". Apart from the symbolism of "Polish-Soviet friendship", the location was symbolic too. The Palace was built in the city center, where part of it was located within the boundaries of the former Jewish quarter of Warsaw.

Fig.2-4 Palace of Culture and Science under construction. Completed in 1956, the palace became one of the most widely recognized sites/symbols of Warsaw.

Setting aside urban developments, why did the city's reconstruction matter for composing a national narrative about the past? After all, other regions of Poland were also affected by World War II. Moreover, other regions had their local collective memories, their local narratives of history. One of the possible explanations is perhaps connected with the impact World War II had on Warsaw and Poland. The interwar Polish Republic was, by large, a decentralized country. Regional identities and everyday lives were shaped by local capitals. The city of Poznań dominated the Greater Poland region and Western Poland in general, Vilnius was influential for the country's northeast, Lwow in the southeast. One could also mention Kraków—the old capital of Poland, which during the time of partition rivaled Warsaw as a home for Polish intelligentsia. World War II did change everything: Vilnius and Lwow became incorporated into the USSR whereas the role of other centers was to be marginalized. At the same time, the centralized nature of the Poland People's Republic elevated Warsaw's status. Poland's capital reconstruction became a national matter. Here, we may go one step further and claim that Warsaw collective memory became a matter for the national narrative.

Likewise, developments in the national historical narratives manifested more clearly than before in the Warsaw landscape. What was interesting is that one of the first monuments erected in Warsaw after 1945 was not connected with the local experience of the War. Neither the Warsaw Ghetto Uprising of 1943 nor the Warsaw Uprising of 1944 were the topic of the statue. This monument, the "Brotherhood of Arms Monument" [Fig.2-5] was referring to the same idea as the Palace of Culture and Science contained, the idea of imagined brotherhood between the Soviets and the Poles.

Fig.2-5 Brotherhood of Arms Monument (Pomnik Braterstwa Broni), one of the earliest monuments erected in post-war Warsaw.

The caption on the monument read: "Long live heroes of the Soviet Army. For Brothers of Arms, who sacrificed their lives for freedom and independence of Polish Nation. Warsaw inhabitants raised this monument." Thus we may see that Brotherhood of Arms was pointing to broader narrative—a reference to Warsaw being a secondary one. Naturally, soon more localized commemorations appeared. In 1946, a small tablet was erected to the memory of Soldiers of the Polish 1st Army landing on the left bank of the Vistula River—an event which was briefly described in Chapter One. The event was the remember as the "Czerniaków landing"—as the landing and subsequent combat occurred in an area known as Czerniaków. In 1951, at the peak of the Stalinism period, another, larger memorial was presented to the public [Fig.2-6]. The tablet was to commemorate "troops of the 3rd Infantry Division of the Polish Army supported by artillery and Soviet aviation—rushing to help the fighting people of Warsaw." as a result of "an unequal battle with the overwhelming forces of the Nazi army". According to the tablet, this resulted in the following casualties: "2,056 soldiers and officers of the Polish Army and Soviet Army, and hundreds of insurgents from of Czerniaków and Solec". Once again, the emphasis was placed on Polish-Soviet military cooperation.

Fig.2-6 The Czerniaków landing commemoration. The plaque was one of the first commemorations of the event.

These attempts, whether it was reconstructing the Old Town, building the Palace of Culture and Science, or unveiling the Brotherhood of Arms monument, could be loosely linked with concepts of cultural studies researcher Marcin Napiórkowski. In his work *Uprising of the Dead (Powstanie Umarłych)*, he used the category of a topos; its difference from the narrative category is a subtle one. Based on Ernst Robert Curtius' definition, Napiórkowski described topos as "a set of pre-made templates, which are comprehensible both for speakers and listeners, used in telling stories (histories)". Such stories, Napiórkowski stressed, had to be "understandable (for speakers and listeners)" and "meaningful" (that is, conveying particular meaning). These templates are not simply what is written or spoken; they can be complex forms of expression: "certain ways of imaging, seeing, acting".

Here, Napiórkowski distinguished "the march topos" (pol. topos pochodu) and a more traditional "cortege topos". The cortege (funeral procession, pol. topos konduktu) emphasized the importance of mourning the dead and was linked with notions of Polish martyrdom. It also had a psychological aspect too: by working through the trauma, engaging with it, one could build a healthier relationship with the present and the future. The march had a different overtone. Contrary to the cortege, which focuses on the past, the march always looks to the future. If the cortege wanted to work through the trauma, the march narrative offered to leave the trauma behind. Considering Poland and Warsaw during World War II, the march topos would probably describe their experience in the following way: Even though the Poles had to sacrifice a lot during World War II, they nevertheless proved victorious for the struggle against fascism. Now, the new government was to construct a new socialist order. Yes, Warsaw was destroyed, but the city rose from its ashes and was looking forward to new developments.

The issue remained on how to shape past war experiences to fit such topos—or narrative, to simplify the matter. For the September Campaign and the Warsaw city defense, a solution could be the following proposition: Even if the *sanacja* government was not a progressive one and was far from being socialist ideal, nevertheless, the people of Warsaw stood together in their fight against the German occupants. That is to say, the very first days of war witnessed the heroism of ordinary city inhabitants which stayed in contrast to the incompetence of the pre-war government.

Now, there was the question of the Warsaw Ghetto Uprising of 1943. Compared to the Warsaw Uprising of 1944, the Warsaw Ghetto Uprising proved in some ways to be less problematic to be remembered. As Ewa Sztompke described, commemoration came as early as 1946, during the third anniversary of the Warsaw Ghetto Uprising. The monument designed by Leon Suzin was placed in Muranów district, nearby Zamenhof Street. It consists of two parts that resemble sewer manholes. The first part was built into the pavement and engraved with two symbols: a letter "B" which "comes from the Hebrew word bereszit (in the beginning), the first word of Genesis". The cast iron leaf symbolizes the martyrdom of Jewish fighters. The second part concentrated on a memory tablet. Its inscription states the following passage: "19.04.1946—For those who fell in an unexceptional fight for dignity and freedom of the Jewish Nation, for free Poland and the humankind liberation—Polish Jews." An inscription was written in three languages: Polish, Yiddish, and Hebrew. [Fig.2-7]

In 1948, during the fifth anniversary of the Warsaw Ghetto Uprising, a considerably larger monument was unveiled. Sculpted by Nathan Rappaport, the second monument took a rectangular shape. The frontal facade depicted Jewish fighters, one of them being insurgency commander Mordechai Anielewicz. One may observe the caption in Polish, Hebrew, and Yiddish language: "The Jewish Nation—for their fighters and martyrs." [Fig.2-8] The rear facade featured a "death march scene, showing the Jews being led to the Treblinka Death Camp".

Fig.2-7 The Monument to the Ghetto Heroes of 1946. It is commonly known as the first monument—in contrast to the larger memorial unveiled two years later.

Both monuments were well received by the audience—both architecture specialists and the insurgents themselves. In addition, there were two things which made these monuments exceptional. First, it was their narrative; it differed from the later Holocaust narrative. For Ghetto Heroes Monument(s), Jewish people were presented as heroic fighters: not just as people who were killed brutally, but who took their arms and fought against the Germans. By contrast, the Holocaust narrative mostly centers on the Jewish experience of World War II as that of an innocent victim, a civilian killed during mass extermination. The second unusual thing about these monuments was the time of their construction. Starting from 1948, the government policies became more Soviet-oriented, so did the narrative. To put it simply, the period between 1945 and 1948 was the last time when the construction of these monuments was possible.

Fig.2-8 The Monument to the Ghetto Heroes of 1948, also known as the second monument. The photo shows the main sculpture of the monument's front side.

The Warsaw Uprising had far less luck to be remembered in this period. Many questions appeared: how to remember the death of 200,000 Poles, most of them being civilians? How to evaluate the resistance movement at the time? The new government represented by the PPR and PZPR (from 1948 onwards) had to face an additional problem. The Uprising itself was militarily against the German army, but it was also perceived as being against the interests of the USSR. Even though the Uprising was foremost a tragedy to Warsaw people, remembering and writing about the event was inherently politicized.

As the first commemoration of the Uprising took place in 1945, the main tenants of the dominant narrative were set. At its early stage, it was agreed that remembering those who fought against the Germans should be important—regardless of different opinions about the Uprising. At the same time, those who fought in the Uprising and who were aligned with the pro-Soviet resistance were elevated within the narrative. Among them, soldiers of the People's Army (Armia Ludowa, the AL) stood out at that time. Formed in 1944 as the military organization of the Polish Workers Party, the AL was a force distinct from the Home Army—the dominant resistance organization. People's Army soldiers fought in the 1944 Uprising and organized partisan actions across German-occupied Poland. After the war, the AL received its official cemetery quarters [Fig.2-9].

Fig.2-9 Powązki Military Cemetery, Quarters of the People's Army (Armia Ludowa), one of the earliest quarters built for particular resistance organizations after World War II.

Despite the AL being substantially smaller than the AK, it could be perceived as the leading force of the resistance. This was partially due to the symbolic prevalence of commemorations dedicated to the AL in public space. An example could be one of many plaques commemorating the People's Guards (Gwardia Ludowa) [Fig.2-10]. Formed in 1942, the Guards were the predecessor of the AL. In 1952, during the 10th anniversary of the Polish Workers Party and the People's Guards formation, plaques were unveiled in various areas in Warsaw. Apart from commemorations, the AL combatants became the backbone of veteran institutions. In 1949, the governmental representatives formed the Society of Fighters for Freedom and Democracy (Związek Bojowników o Wolność i Demokrację, ZBoWiD). During the time of its functioning, especially at the time of Stalinism, it focused on accepting combatants representing pro-Soviet organizations, including the People's Army combatants and former soldiers of the Polish Army formed in the East.

Fig.2-10 A plaque dedicated to the People's Guards. Between 1942 and 1943, its soldiers attacked the "Hitlerite" Cafe Club in Warsaw—in retaliation for actions against the resistance.

Compared with the People's Army, the Home Army veterans were not to be treated with the same appraisal. Between 1945 and 1956, the attitude of the new government was largely hostile: former AK members were perceived as a potential threat to the new order. Soon after the War ended, many of the Home Army high-ranked officers were caught by the intelligence forces and being sentenced either in Warsaw or in Moscow, USSR. Some of the prominent resistance leaders received the death penalty and/or were tortured throughout their stay in jails. The state of active hostility towards the AK or other organizations related to it continued until 1956. In official media and culture at the time, members of the AK were labeled as "bandits" and their contributions to the resistance were largely omitted.

The only exception when some commemorations with AK veterans took place, was in the period between 1945 and 1946. As Marcin Napiórkowski described, the first anniversary of the Warsaw Rising was celebrated on the 1st of August 1945. During memorials conducted at the Powązki Military Cemetery, government officials representing main political factions praised the brotherhood of the People's Army and the Home Army soldiers in the common fight against the fascist enemy. They honored the "heroic people of Warsaw" for their bravery displayed during the War. At the same time, governmental politicians, as well as the official press which commented on the anniversary, pointed to the "usurpers", who wanted to steal the Uprising for their cause. These usurpers would be associated with leaders of the Home Army and representatives of the London Government.

Apart from the state-organized commemorations, Warsaw inhabitants themselves organized their activities. During that period the division between official and non-official celebrations crystalized— the governmental side organized activities at the Military Cemetery whereas the non-official celebrations were held at Old Powązki Cemetery, where some of the insurgents were already buried. The official and non-official dimensions clashes pretty much followed a conflict between the march topos and the cortege topos, respectively.

The problem of commemorating the Warsaw Uprising was not limited to organizing anniversaries. It was also about creating statues, plaques, and other—smaller or larger—sites of memory/memory mediums. In 1946, Gloria Victis Monument was unveiled at Powązki Military Cemetery as part of the initiative proposed by the insurgents [Fig.2-11]. As Marcin Napiórkowski noted, "the Gloria Victis was not a monument in a strict sense but rather an extension of already existing site of memory to the fallen" . Jacek Sawicki in his publication "Battle for the Truth" (*Bitwa o pamięć*) described the statue in the broader context of a "memory struggle" between former insurgents and the government of the Polish People's Republic. He described the statue in the following way: "The monument was shaped in a form of a squared obelisk from black granite, completed with an urn. On four sides of the granite, bronze inscriptions were placed, including 'Warsaw Uprising 1st August—2nd October 1944'." Other sides contained: an inscription "Gloria Victis" (Glory to the defeated), a sign of the Fighting Poland Anchor placed together with dates 1939-1945. Last, but not least, the remaining part contained the following sentence: "For Soldiers of the Home Army and for the fallen in fighting for liberty – their comrades in arms."

The Gloria Victis Statue was one of the first commemorations related to the Warsaw Uprising. That being said, it was not called "the Warsaw Uprising Monument" as any direct reference to 1944 insurgency was impossible at the time. The statue was an initiative of colonel Jan Mazurkiewicz (nom de guerre "Radosław"), one of the main protectors of the AK veterans community after the War. Despite growing persecutions, "Radosław" did his best to provide aid to former soldiers of the Home Army. For his activities, he was arrested in 1949, the year which marked the peak of the Stalinism period in Poland.

Fig.2-11 Gloria Victis Monument at Powązki Military Cemetery. The front of the statue contained a visible "Fighting Anchor" symbol and dates signifying World War II: 1939-1945.

The state continued to implement new practices of memory, sometimes by modifying existing customs. One was a practice of Warsaw inhabitants to honor the fallen by placing small crosses. So far, we focused more on commemorations of people associated with combatant organizations: the Home Army, the People's Army, and narrative clashes connected with them. However, we should note that not all victims were armed combatants. Many of them were civilians, among which some lost their lives during the 1944 Rising. Others died out of other causes. They were those who were caught by the German occupant at the time when their troops were engaged in combat with resistance forces. Some were executed publicly—ofttimes in an act of retaliation. During the War and immediately after it, circumstances made it impossible to provide organized funerals to all the deceased. Maciej Janaszek Seydlitz in his work regarding the future Warsaw Uprising cemetery described the atmosphere in post-war Warsaw: "A forest of crosses on makeshift graves stood out from under the snow.

On streets and in ruins lied unburied bodies, and in many places, the wind blew away human ashes which accumulated on tall, macabre piles."

The custom was modified: crosses were to be replaced by state-sponsored tablets. Every tablet would commemorate a site where multiple deceased were killed—either over time or during a single event. Its architect, Karol Tchorek, won the project, whose designed tablets featured a Maltan cross with inscriptions placed on it. Tchorek's original idea was to depict the way Warsaw people commemorated their fallen relatives and friends as loyal to the original as he could. Soon after his project was selected, the construction began. Today, there are about 100 plaques throughout Warsaw, making them a particular type of element in the city's landscape [Fig.2-12].

These were initial developments in post-war memory and narrative building. The dominant narrative was constructed and its initial tenants were as follows: the People's Army, fighting along with the Home Army and Warsaw people, having aid from the Red Army, fought bravely against forces of the Germans.

Fig.2-12 One of many Tchorek's Plaques. The one presented in the photo commemorated victims killed in Headquarters of the Gestapo, Nazi Germany Secret Police.

105

A Stabilized Narrative

The death of Joseph Stalin in 1953 and subsequent rise to power by Nikita Khrushchev was a sign to countries of the Soviet Bloc that there would be a shift in policies. In Poland, Władysław Gomułka steadily grew his support and eventually became the First Secretary of the PZPR in 1956. The official rhetoric around the Home Army softened and some of its former leaders, including Jan Mazurkiewicz "Radosław", were released from prison. The period, which is many times described as "the October Thaw", was the period of political liberalization.

As for Warsaw and its narrative of history, it meant that one may once again discuss more freely the past events. One also may notice the generational shift which happened during that period. Now, the youngest adults were mostly children during the Warsaw Uprising. On the other hand, the insurgents were slightly older, usually in their late 20s or early 30s. This period, although being short, brought some changes within the narrative. Monuments from that period indicate this shift. The Czerniaków landing, which was commemorated with a plaque in 1951, was remembered with a new statue built in 1957 [Fig.2-13]. Compared to its predecessor, it stressed more participation of the Home Army troops in the event.

Fig.2-13 Monument to Czerniaków Insurgents and Soldiers of the 1st Polish Army. Its inscription mentions detachments of the Home Army and People's Army as well as civilians killed in 1944.

The shift was not simply a matter of monuments. In general, the subject of war was discussed more freely by the veterans, especially among Warsaw Uprising insurgents. Since the end of the War, many of them were collecting materials—documents, history books, and popular literature—for the sake of better understanding the past events [Fig.2-14]. For the larger public, the War was also the subject of literature and film. Two films by Polish director Andrzej Wajda, *Kanał* (Sewer, 1956) and *Popiół i Diament* (Ashes and Diamonds, 1958) offered a more nuanced approach towards the subject of the War, relations of different groups within the resistance as well as the post-war order. Władysław Zambrzycki published in 1959 his prose *Kwatera Bożych Pomyleńców* (Quarter of Godly Lunatics), which offered a unique perspective on 1944 Rising. For Zambrzycki, the Uprising was not only the domain of young combat veterans but also an everyday life struggle for civilians, who sometimes were not fit to join militarily the Uprising.

Fig.2-14 Warsaw insurgent Tadeusz Wóycicki's personal collection of books concerning the Warsaw Uprising, under the courtesy of his son Kazimierz Wóycicki.

The October Thaw, as it will be later called in historiography, was, however, a brief period. Two factors contributed to it: one was the rising opposition to Gomułka's rule, which demanded more radical political reforms. Young party members and journalists, gathered around the journal *Po Prostu*, represented a voice of the new generation. The second main factor was the Hungarian Revolution of 1956. Hungarian Prime Minister Imre Nagy declared his country neutral and took it out of the Warsaw Pact. This resulted in Soviet Intervention in November 1956.

In 1957, the political climate in the country changed. After seizing and consolidating his power, Władysław Gomułka started to withdraw from his promises for the reforms. The same year, the journal *Po Prostu* was closed and the position of Gomułka within the party strengthened. Poland was about to enter the period of the so-called small stabilization, which encompassed the entire rule of Gomułka as the first secretary from 1956 to 1970. The small stabilization period offered a less oppressive political system. That also meant partial rehabilitation for the Home Army Members. Warsaw Uprising celebrations were tolerated, most notably at Powązki. The new period marked the shift within the generation. The wartime generation (people born in the 1920s) became middle-aged people, whereas their children (born in the 1940s) started to enter adulthood. The new generation also had to face the problem of remembering the difficult past.

Despite limited reforms, the October Thaw opened up a space for a new discussion concerning the Uprising. Works of Jerzy Kirchmayer are a good example of this trend. Kirchmayer, originally a soldier of the Second Republic, became a member of the AK at the time of occupation. Later on, he joined Polish People's Army, Poland's official armed forces between 1945 and 1989. Here, he reached the rank of brigade general in 1947. During his final years (he died in 1959), Kirchmayer managed to prepare his synthesis entitled *Powstanie Warszawskie* (Warsaw Uprising), where he offered a comprehensive study of the armed conflict and mostly focused on the military aspect of the Uprising. The period also saw some more specialist studies. Tadeusz Klimaszewski's *Verbrennungskommando Warschau* dealt with a topic of Warsaw burning detachment. The *Verbrennungskommando* was a slave labor unit formed by the Nazi Germany *Schutzschtaffel* (the SS—a paramilitary organization of the Nazi Party) following the Wola massacre in the early days of the 1944 Uprising. Its role was to remove evidence of perpetrated massacres by the occupants. In another study *Z pomocą powstańcom warszawskim* (Aiding Warsaw Insurgents) Józef Margules discussed the aid provided to the insurgents by the Polish Army, which at the time resided on the right side of the Vistula River.

Changes in the official narrative could be noticed as well. The term "heroes of Warsaw" gained popularity during this period. The figure was used when describing the insurgents, but it could also be interpreted as the tribute to other people—soldiers fighting during the September 1939 campaign, the Ghetto insurgents, the Warsaw insurgents (of all political orientations), the soldiers of the Polish Army fighting in the East, who entered Warsaw in January 1945. The other change was the popularity of the "Grunwald" symbol. Grunwald is an important place in Polish history. In 1410, on the fields nearby Grunwald village, the Kingdom of Poland fought against the medieval Teutonic Order in the war over supremacy in the region. What is important in this story is perhaps not the reference to medieval history, but rather a national perspective that interpreted the conflict as the struggle between different ethnicities: the Poles on one hand, and the Germans on the other.

Fig.2-15 Monument to the Warsaw Heroes 1939-1945. Originally located at the Theater Square, the statue now is placed next to Warsaw W-Z (West-East) route.

But why this reference to the Germans? If we look at early post-war memorials, we see references made to the Germans, the nation itself. But, starting from 1948, the narrative shifted towards the term "Hitlerites". After the destalinization of 1956, the ideological explanation within the narrative still existed but faded. In turn, the national explanation once again was visible and used interchangeably with the ideological one. When talking about the war, one may say it was a war against "German fascism". It also reflected the political nature of the time, when the relations between the Polish People's Republic and the Western German Federal Republic were not normalized. Having in mind these two tendencies, it is easier to understand the "Monument to the Warsaw Heroes 1939-1945" which was built in 1964 [Fig.2-15].

The statue depicts Nike—goddess of victory, holding a giant Grunwald sword and being oriented to the West—the place where the fascist invaders came. In a way, the monument was a blend of narratives. It did not directly mention the Warsaw Uprising, but rather was designed to commemorate all the heroes—of Warsaw city defense, the resistance in general, and Soviet/Polish forces which liberated Warsaw on 17th January 1945.

Another place was getting its relevance for Warsaw collective memory: Pawiak. The name comes from Pawia Street, where the jail was constructed in the 1830s. During the time of the Russian Empire, the jail was for both criminal and political prisoners where the second group became dominant. The Pawiak Prison continued operating in the interwar period—with a change happening during the War. After October 1939, the German occupants started to place here new political prisoners: the Polish intelligentsia, members of the resistance, the Jews, and many others. Many of them were subjects of brutal torture and executions, which became well known in the entire city.

For its grim fame, the Pawiak eventually became a target for the resistance. In March 1943, a group of soldiers of the Home Army implemented Operation Arsenal. Some of the political prisoners, who were being transferred to Pawiak, were successfully liberated. One month later, the Warsaw Ghetto Uprising started. The prison was gradually abandoned, its prisoners mostly relocated to other detention facilities or concentration camps, some executed in the prison. The last guards of Pawiak left it in late August 1944, at the time when the Warsaw Uprising had already begun. After the War, only two objects remained from the original prison—the white elm tree and a part of the main gate. The elm tree became the place where families of prisoners would place a small tablet to remember the victims.

In 1964, the museum was opened to the public [Fig.2-16]. In a similar way to the Heroes of Warsaw Monument, the Pawiak Prison Museum points directly to the existence of the German Occupants. Moreover, both sites of memory were dedicated to different groups of people. As we said, the Warsaw Heroes Monument commemorated September 1939 soldiers, two uprisings combatants, and many others. The Pawiak Museum commemorated various prisoners: some of them being ethnically Polish, some were Jewish. Some of the prisoners were civilians whereas the others were soldiers of the resistance movement.

This diversity of prisoners also posed another question: how to portray the perpetrator/victim dimension? At the time the museum was opened to the public, the Holocaust narrative, which presented Jewish people as the pure victims, became the predominant one. Yet the Pawiak story presented a more complex picture—people of both nationalities (Polish and Jewish) sometimes being "pure victims" (mostly civilians), sometimes being "militant victims" (mostly soldiers of the resistance).

Speaking of the Jewish community, despite suffering heavy losses and migration during the War, Polish Jews managed to restore remnants of their community in post-war Warsaw. Former insurgents of the Warsaw Ghetto after destalinization continued commemorations of their Uprising [Fig.2-17]. Yet there were several growing problems which affected heavily Polish-Jewish relations. When the post-war Polish state was organized in 1945, it originally maintained good contacts with local and global Jewish communities. Celebrations of the Ghetto were held and some ethnic Jewish people were involved in the post-war government. However, the situation changed when an independent Israeli state was formed in 1948. As time passed, Israel was increasingly more aligned with the United States, the main rival of the USSR during the Cold War.

Fig.2-16 The Pawiak Prison Museum. The main gate of the prison, and the elm tree described above, are both visible in the photo.

Fig.2-17 Ceremony at the Monument of the Ghetto Heroes. The photo was included in a monograph commemorating the 20th anniversary of the insurgency.

At the time of Władysław Gomułka's tenure as the First Secretary of the Polish United Workers Party, a new influential group appeared: the so-called Partisans. Its leader Mieczysław Moczar proposed integrating Polish society around the combatant tradition of Poland. Such a narrative was promoted by Zbigniew Załuski, one of the popular historians who was associated with the movement. Unlike Stalinist politicians before, the Partisans perceived Home Army soldiers not as "bandits", but rather as a part of the same patriotic front which secured Polish independence. Since the AK was not considered an enemy, politicians of the Partisan faction pointed to the Jews instead. In their eyes, Jewish people could not be trusted as representatives of a foreign nation.

Such rhetoric became even more visible after the Six Days War between Israel and Arab countries in 1967. Moczar and its faction claimed that there was a "fifth column" in Poland which represented Jewish interests. During the same period, students of Warsaw University and Warsaw Technical University began showing their increasing dissent. All those tendencies escalated in what was later to be known as the "March Events" of 1968. Massive demonstrations were held, many Polish Jews decided to leave the country. Relations between Poland and the Jewish community were shattered. Jews in Warsaw and Poland greatly limited their activities and the situation did not change until 1989.

The March Events eventually led to a power struggle between the Partisans and Władysław Gomułka. Despite Gomułka emerging victorious, he did not hold onto power for too long. Following workers strikes of December 1970, he was replaced by Edward Gierek who became the new First Secretary of the PUWP.

The rise of Edward Gierek marked a new chapter in contemporary Polish history. Gierek, who presented himself as a young dynamic leader compared to aging Gomułka, promised a modernization program that the country needed.

Warsaw city landscape was affected by new constructions made by the government. New housing estates built with the usage of the grand plate technology mushroomed across the capital. The government also made one symbolic gesture which was important at that time. It approved a total reconstruction of the Royal Castle.

The Castle was not rebuilt directly after the war. In 1949, the Sejm formally passed the resolution to rebuild this royal residence. It was, however, rather a symbolic gesture. The postwar Capital Reconstruction Bureau and the local/central authorities, in general, were focused on reconstructing other places (including the Old Town) or building new ones. The site around the Royal Castle was secured, but the date of full reconstruction was postponed. Luckily, an impulse came in 1964, when the Castle's ruins were enlisted as the UNESCO World Heritage Site. Later on, Gierek's modernization program addressed a commonly shared desire to rebuild the Royal Castle. For many, it remained one of the most important symbols of Warsaw and Polish statehood. Therefore, the reconstruction process started in 1971 and was completed in 1984. [Fig.2-18]

The reconstruction was an achievement for Warsaw local architecture. But perhaps a symbolic aspect of the endeavor was equally important. A site of memory was (re)created: Royal Castle in Warsaw, which was left in ruins even after the War ended, now presented itself fully restored. One could even argue that it was the biggest contribution of the Gierek decade. In terms of commemoration and historical narrative, the period was not innovative too much as for the narrative and it generally followed the principles established earlier.

Fig.2-18 The Royal Castle in Warsaw under reconstruction with its front side being visible. The photo was taken in 1974.

Take the example of the September Barricade Monument (Pomnik Barykady Września), which was publicly displayed in 1979 [Fig.2-19]. That year marked the 40th anniversary beginning of the War as well as the beginning of the Warsaw siege. The September Barricade is a concrete form depicting the dates of the city defense (8 IX – 27 IX 1939). The caption stated that the Polish Army fought hand in hand with Warsaw inhabitants against forces of Hitlerites. What is interesting here is the usage of the word Hitlerites once again (and not the Germans) as not pointing to the nationality of the invader. The other is the lack of usage of the phrase "Warsaw People" in favor of "Warsaw inhabitants". The former phrase was frequently used until the end of the Gomułka period.

Apart from the Warsaw defense of 1939, other episodes were given attention to. This included the Czerniaków landing, which memorization started directly in postwar Poland. However, the memorization added new elements to be remembered. An interesting example of it is the Glory to the Sappers Monument which was unveiled in 1975 [Fig.2-20]. Located in the vicinity of existing plaques and statues, this memorial linked Czerniaków landing with deeds of sappers conducted after the War ended. In a way, we could say that the site of memory that Czerniaków became was enriched with new elements, new memory mediums.

Fig.2-19 The September Barricade Monument. The photo features part of the memorial with the date of 8th September presented in a barricade-like concrete form.

Fig.2-20 Glory to the Sappers Monument. After Warsaw liberation in January 1945, the sappers made toilsome efforts to dispose of remaining explosives within the city.

Naturally, we remember that the Czerniaków landing was also a part of memory about the Warsaw Uprising. Since Czerniakow-related memorials appeared during the Gierek decade, it is not surprising that the insurgency was commemorated as well. The subject of the Warsaw Uprising was visible in literature and films of the time. In 1970, Polish poet Miron Białoszewski published his *Memoir from the Warsaw Uprising* (*Pamiętnik Powstania Warszawskiego*). This was the voice of a person who witnessed the Rising as a civilian rather than a combatant. Another piece of literature, *Kamienie na szaniec* by Alexander Kaminski, which was originally written in 1943, received its second life. It inspired the making of the film *Akcja pod Arsenałem* (*Operation Arsenal*). Directed in 1977, the film was centered its plot around actions performed by Zośka batallion of the Home Army, which aimed at liberating their fellow soldiers before their transfer to the infamous Pawiak Prison.

Despite being a subject of literature and films, the Home Army was still waiting for its bigger tribute from the authorities. Information about their veterans was blurry and often censored, many times put in a very general "insurgent" category. That being said, the official stance towards the Home Army softened. The usage of the word "bandits", which was frequently attributed to the Home Army Supreme Command, gradually diminished. Consequently, a gradual shift in the narrative became possible. For the 35th anniversary of the Warsaw Uprising in 1979, the Warsaw Insurgents Monument was unveiled [Fig.2-21]. It was one of the major commemorations of the Warsaw Uprising during the Gierek decade—marking the transition period to the 1980s. The memorial symbolized such a transition: it still commemorated "the insurgents" and not the "Warsaw Uprising" in its name. As Marcin Napiórkowski noted: such a difference "seems to be minor, but both for the authorities and the initiators of this construction—it was significant".

Fig.2-21 The Warsaw Insurgents Monument. Its inscription specifically commemorates the Home Army Battalion "Kiliński" which engaged in combat on 1st August 1944, at the beginning of the Warsaw Uprising.

The discussion about memory and historiography of the Warsaw Uprising during the 1970s was not limited only to Poland. The Polish diaspora was also interested in the narrative building, however, due to political circumstances, their voice was largely separate from the Polish People's Republic government. Since 1945, the Polish Government in Exile rallied the Polish diaspora within the United Kingdom which comprised many former World War II veterans. These included the Home Army High Command as well as a substantial number of Warsaw insurgents. Among them, Jan Ciechanowski, a former participant of the Warsaw Uprising, wrote his study on the conflict. Ciechanowski had an opportunity to use sources that were hardly available back in Poland, including memoirs and interviews with the Home Army High Command leaders. He noted that the resistance soldiers were hardly prepared for the upcoming battle.

Back in Gierek's Poland, local historians continued studies on the Warsaw Uprising. There were more, however, concerned with filling white spots. In other words, they were discussing the remaining subjects considering the Uprising rather than with radical changes for the narrative. They followed study cases that were done before; Zbigniew Woźniewski's work on the medical treatment during the Uprising being a notable example of such tendency. Major changes had to happen in the next decade after the downfall of Edward Gierek.

The Narrative Shift during the Time of Changes

In the late 1970s, Gierek's government faced emerging economic difficulties. The government had to respond by cutting spending and raising the prices of consumer goods. This combined with social unrest resulted in the formation of opposition which eventually evolved into the Solidarity (Solidarność) movement of the 1980s. On the governmental side, Edward Gierek was replaced first by Stanisław Kania and finally by general Wojciech Jaruzelski.

General Jaruzelski, born in 1920, was connected before with the faction of Partisans. As a young adult, he enlisted himself in Polish Army in the East under General Zygmunt Berling. Together with fellow soldiers, he fought back his way to Poland. In the 1960s he was noticed by the Minister of Interior Mieczysław Moczar and he was appointed as the new Minister of Defense.

At first glance, Jaruzelski shared with the Partisans his military past. But unlike Moczar, he was not a member of the communist guerilla and was serving in the regular army. In addition, his upbringing was more similar to members of former noble families and that of the intelligentsia. Where as Moczar was coming from a family of mostly peasant origins, Jaruzelski's family included noblemen who took part in national uprisings, for instance, his grandfather fighting in the January Rising of 1863.

Because of his background, Jaruzelski had a more favorable opinion regarding former Polish military traditions. This included the interwar Polish military as well as the Home Army formed at the time of resistance. Where the Partisans still accented the role of the People's Army and pro-Soviet forces, Jaruzelski watered down this element in favor of a more friendly approach towards the Home Army. The acknowledgment many years after the War was put into practice. Jan Mazurkiewicz "Radosław", the very same person who had to face Stalinist repressions, was promoted to the rank of brigade general in October 1980. On 1st August 1981, on the 37th anniversary of the Warsaw Uprising, Mazurkiewicz and other 100 people were awarded the Warsaw Uprising Cross.

The insurgents started working on establishing Warsaw Rising Museum and on statue commemorations. This included the Little Insurgent Monument (Pomnik Małego Powstańca) built in 1983 [Fig.2-22]. The role of the monument was to commemorate the youngest of the insurgents. The monument can be linked to the debate on the role of the insurgency for the youngest generations—people who experienced the conflict as adolescents. Supporters of the Uprising described the enthusiasm of its youngest participants whereas opponents pointed out the loss of innocent lives.

Fig.2-22 The Little Insurgent Monument, unveiled in 1983.

Soon, the discussion about erecting the Warsaw Uprising Monument became a hot topic. During that time, Mazurkiewicz was a member of the ZBoWiD combatant organization commission responsible for building it. Even though "Radosław" was not able to see the monument (he died in 1988), its construction was finally put into practice. The Warsaw Uprising Monument (Pomnik Powstania Warszawskiego) was erected in 1989 [Fig.2-23]. The period was also important for the insurgents. Senior commanders of the uprising were either in very advanced age or already deceased. Younger officers and soldiers also aged significantly, most of them being over 60 years old. The second generation was already mature and the third generation (that is, grandchildren of the insurgents) was emerging. Therefore, it was the period where the continuity of the memory was still present.

Fig.2-23 The Warsaw Uprising Monument is the main part of the sculpture. The monument depicts a group of insurgents who are taking cover. The rear part resembles both ruins of the Old Town and city sewer canals.

The monument thus appeared where three generations (witnesses of the Uprising, their children, and grandchildren) finally appeared. It was a full and direct commemoration of the Uprising since it explicitly pointed out the event itself. Marcin Napiórkowski noted that technically speaking, the Warsaw Uprising Monument was originally accepted under the name of "Heroes of the Warsaw Uprising". However, the usage of this name was discontinued. Today the monument is simply known as the "Warsaw Uprising Monument" today. Thus I decided to simplify the matter here.

Up to this moment, we could see three similar memorials: the 1964 Warsaw Heroes Monument, the 1979 Warsaw Insurgents Monument, and the 1989 Warsaw Uprising Monument. Since they were built at different times, three memorials express different motivations behind their construction as well as pointing out different elements of collective memory.

Until the 1960s, the governmental side was not willing to accept the historic importance of the Warsaw Uprising for Poland's war efforts. The government even referred to the insurgents (its commanders or the Home Army members) as "bandits". For this reason, it refrained from making direct memorization of the Warsaw Uprising or insurgents themselves. Thus the government opted for the "Warsaw Heroes" figure which commemorated all those who took part in defending Warsaw. In the 1970s, even though the topic of the Warsaw Uprising was still controversial and the discussion regarding whether or not the decision to launch the insurgency was justified continued, the insurgents themselves were increasingly seen as someone who should be venerated. Thus we may observe a shift from "Warsaw Heroes" to "Warsaw Insurgents" figures. However, the Home Army veterans were in a way incorporated into the broader category of "insurgents". It was only in the 1980s when, through efforts of influential people such as Jaruzelski and "Radosław", the Warsaw Uprising received its memorial. In other words, this monument was explicitly commemorating the insurgency. By these means, soldiers fighting under the Home Army finally received full recognition for their actions conducted during the War.

Such a revision of the narrative was a risky measurement for Jaruzelski. As Marcin Napiórkowski pointed out, the Warsaw Uprising commemoration had its anti-system nature. During the 1980s, commemorative activities many times turned into political manifestations against the government. The insurgents were perceived as those who were fighting to free an independent Poland, the one which will not be dominated by external powers. Such an unofficial narrative challenged the government legitimacy that had its grounding in the international situation. The "march" narrative emphasized the Polish-Soviet alliance against the potential German revisionism. However, as we are going to describe later, the Poles and the Germans made significant progress in reconciliation during the 1960s and the 1970s. As a result, the international source of legitimacy for the governmental rule started to be undermined. An increasing acceptance for the commemoration of the Uprising did not help either. Apart from gaining recognition, former insurgents spoke freely about the past. Their words ofttimes undermined the official narrative built after 1945. The "march" was about to crumble.

The changes were also visible in the approach of Jewish community memorization, for instance regarding the "Umschlagplatz" site of memory. The term meant a reloading square, a place where the Jews living in the Ghetto were waiting for the train—officially to be "relocated", unofficially to be sent to the Treblinka Death Camp. The place became one of the most important sites of memory for the Jewish community. Thus, it was a natural decision to build a monument that would pay a tribute to the victims.

Fig.2-24 The Umschlagplatz Memorial. The main white marble component together with the bronze tablet on the top is visible in the photo.

In 1988, during the 45th anniversary of the Warsaw Ghetto Uprising and 20 years after the March of 1968, the Umschlagplatz Memorial was presented to the public [Fig.2-24]. The main part of the memorial contains a white marble structure with a bronze tablet over it. As Ewa Sztompke noted, the main part resembles an open freight wagon, whereas the broken forest carving on a bronze tablet symbolized the premature death of the Relocated. The memorial also includes names of people who were taken from Umschlagplatz to death camps and a poem from the *Book of Job*: "Earth, do not cover my blood; may my cry never be laid to rest!" All these elements symbolically refer to the fate of the relocated Jews.

The memorial could be seen as another important milestone in commemorating the fate of the Jewish community in World War II. It presented a different narrative from the one which characterized the Ghetto Heroes Monument of 1948. The older commemoration emphasized the bravery of the Jewish Ghetto insurgents. By contrast, the Umschlagplatz Memorial appeared after the establishment of the Holocaust narrative. Unlike the Ghetto Heroes Monument narrative, the new memorial presented the Jews as victims foremost.

The 1980s was a time of transformation for Warsaw collective memory and the narrative of history.

The period after 1989 brought changes to the narrative present in Warsaw. On one hand, the disappearance of the Eastern Bloc meant that some narratives and commemorations of the Polish People's Republic were to be revised or discontinued in the new Third Republic. On the other hand, the period brought a new variety in memorization of the Warsaw past.

Directly after the War, many prominent Home Army senior commanders decided to stay in exile. Many of them resided in London where the so-called Government in Exile continued its functioning. In the 1990s, the Government in Exile welcomed the new authorities of Poland. After symbolically transferring its power to the Third Republic representatives, the London Government officially dissolved. The transition could not be seen by some of the former Home Army leaders who passed away. Among the commanders was general Tadeusz Komorowski, the commandant of the Home Army during the Uprising. However, his ashes were symbolically returned to Poland by his son, and the general was re-buried at Old Powązki Cemetery.

This happened in 1994, during the 50th anniversary of the Warsaw Uprising. The occasion prompted back the topic of building the Warsaw Rising Museum. The cornerstone was set, however, the construction had an unclear law status and it had to be postponed. Meanwhile, the insurgents had to be content with commemorations on a smaller scale. As an example, the Home Army veterans who gave aid to the Czerniaków landing were memorized in a new plaque [Fig.2-25] placed near past monuments.

Speaking of the veterans, their associations were restructured. In 1990, ZBoWiD was transformed into the Polish Society of War Veterans and Former Political Prisoners (Związek Kombatantów RP i Byłych Więźniów Politycznych). One year earlier, the Warsaw insurgents established their organization: the Warsaw Insurgents Association (Związek Powstańców Warszawskich) with Zbigniew Ścibor-Rylski as their first long term president. Ścibor-Rylski graduated as an airman and a warrant officer. When the war started, he served throughout the entire defense campaign of 1939 until its last episode: the battle of Kock (5th October 1939). Later on, he joined the underground resistance as a soldier of the Home Army. In August 1944, Ścibor-Rylski took part in the Uprising. After the War, his superior colonel Jan Mazurkiewicz "Radosław" ordered Ścibor-Rylski to hide his identity as the Home Army Soldier. He thus moved to Poznań, working there as a mechanic. He moved back to Warsaw in the late 1960s after the memorization gradually acknowledged the role of the Home Army. After his retirement in 1977, he became more engaged in commemorations of the Warsaw Uprising. As a member of ZBoWiD, he participated in organizing the 40th anniversary of the Uprising in 1984. Especially after the death of "Radosław", Ścibor-Rylski became increasingly popular among former insurgents. His role as the president of the Warsaw Insurgents Association strengthened his authority.

Fig.2-25 An example of a plaque unveiled in the 1990s, dedicated to Home Army veterans who fought at the Czerniaków area.

Memorization of the Jewish community also had further development. The Jewish Historical Institute, which was established after the War, proposed in 1993 establishing a museum that would commemorate the past of Polish Jews. This also marked the 50th anniversary of the Warsaw Ghetto Uprising. The initiative had its development in 1995 when suitable land was selected for establishing the museum. The same year, a new plaque was placed nearby the Ghetto Heroes Monument. The new plaque was dedicated to the Council to Aid Jews with the Government Delegation for Poland, simply new as "Żegota" [Fig.2-26]. After the Nazi Germany authorities decided on the Final Solution of the Jewish Question, the Polish Underground State, as well as the Polish Government in Exile, were alarmed by the actions of the occupants. As a result, the Council to Aid Jews was formed. Its role included offering help to people inside the Jewish Ghetto. People involved in the organization—such as Władysław Bartoszewski and Irena Sendler—were later conferred by Yad Vashem Institute the title of the Righteous Among Nations.

Fig.2-26 Memorial tablet dedicated to Żegota, the Council to Aid Jews. It lies near Ghetto Heroes Monuments.

Fig.2-27 Stefan Starzyński Monument of 1993. Both this monument and an earlier monument commemorating the president could be interpreted as a sign of approaching the legacy of interwar Warsaw.

Speaking of more individual commemorations, another monument was unveiled in the year 1993, the one dedicated to Stefan Starzyński. Mentioned in Chapter One of this book, Starzyński rose to prominence as a skillful mayor of Warsaw. When the War started in September 1939, Starzyński coordinated civic support for the defense of Warsaw. In 1981, the first monument was dedicated to him. Another monument was unveiled in 1993 [Fig.2-27].

The narrative of the period focused primarily on the Home Army, the Warsaw Uprising, and the fate of the Jewish community. Nevertheless, the period also saw remembrance of other episodes of Polish and Warsaw history. This included the so-called Farmers' Battalions (Bataliony Chłopskie), an armed resistance mostly associated with the Polish People's Party (Polskie Stronnictwo Ludowe, PSL), and with Peasant/Agrarian movement in general. After 1945, the veterans of the Battalions had a similar fate to those of the Home Army veterans, largely being denied any significant commemoration. In 2001, the Battalions received a monument at the Powązki Cemetery [Fig.2-28].

All these discussions happened at a time when Poland was concerned about its future. We may call these tendencies the "Turn to the West". Past experiences were not important at the moment. The 50th anniversary of the Warsaw Uprising in 1994 did not receive similar attention as the 40th anniversary observed in 1984. Part of the reason was that the Poles were preoccupied with integrating with the Western World.

However, not long after, the "Turn to the West" era came to the end. After the accession to North Atlantic Treaty Organization (NATO) in 1997 and the European Union (the EU) in 2004, contemporary leaders of the country fulfilled their political ambitions. However, what was left behind were questions concerning the national identity. The Poles not only did have to answer the question of what they would like to become. The answer to that also needed to conclude the debate on *who we were*. The past resurged itself from being ignored—and it returned with full strength in the next decade.

Fig.2-28 Monument dedicated to Farmers' Battalions. Commemoration of other combatant organizations than the Home Army and the People's Army was a sign of a more pluralist narrative after 1989.

The Resurgence of the Past

The year 2004 marked the accession of Poland into the EU. At the same time, something happened in local politics. In the same year, Lech Kaczyński, who was back then the mayor of Warsaw city, officially announced the opening of the Warsaw Rising Museum. This also marked the 60th anniversary of the Uprising. In terms of remembering the event, it was truly a breakthrough. It also marked the beginning of the new decade in Poland, that is, a decade during which the memory about the past was once again important in public discourse.

One may wonder, why this tendency happened. Several factors contributed to the shift. The first one was the change in politics. Poland successfully integrated itself with structures associated with the West. But now, the question appeared on how to preserve this identity whilst already being in the West. This was even more important if one considers the radical shift that the transformation made to the Polish political system and the everyday lives. It was not possible to maintain the old narrative from the times of Poland before the transformation, nor was it possible to ignore the problem.

The other was the generation shift. Witnesses of the War were already very aged, usually being over 70 years old. Meanwhile, the fourth generation was slowly emerging, that is, people born in the 1990s. This generation could not for obvious reasons remember the War, not to mention the complicated memorization after it. It became crucial then to offer a more coherent and plain narrative about the nation's past. In the Warsaw case, all the experiences of the capital during the War—the city defense in 1939, occupation days, the tale of two uprisings, and the post-war order—had to be retold and reexamined. For many people from the witness generation, it was the last chance to voice out their memories, ofttimes traumatic ones.

The final factor was the institutional basis for the remembering. Two of the planned museums, one for the Warsaw Uprising and one for the Jewish community, had their Committees established earlier. In 1999, the Institute of National Remembrance (Instytut Pamięci Narodowej, the IPN) was formed, and soon it became a major public institution responsible for official narrative building. One might add another factor, that is the role of prominent individuals. Apart from the early mentioned general Ścibor-Rylski, one politician paid a pivotal role in the era—Lech Kaczyński.

Lech Kaczyński, born to a family of Warsaw insurgents, was heavily influenced by his parents considering memorization of the Uprising. When he became mayor of Warsaw in the 2000s, he closely cooperated with the community of insurgents. Kaczyński promised the veterans that for the 60th anniversary of the Uprising, the museum was going to be finished. The promise was made and in 2004, Warsawians could enjoy the new museum Whose history period was so important for local and national identity. Museum benefited from the former Committee's work responsible for the artifacts. The opening of the museum received a lot of attention from scholars and popular culture.

Academics used the opportunity to reexamine the history of Warsaw, Norman Davies' *Rising '44* being a good example of it. Being a new history synthesis towards the Warsaw Uprising, it also covered two additional aspects. One, which came from the author's research, was the international response towards the Warsaw Uprising, that is, why the Allies were so hesitating to provide comprehensive assistance to the insurgents. The other element Davies dealt with was the aftermath of the Uprising till 1956. Apart from *Rising '44*, many new scholarly works were published at that time. It reflected heated debates over the Uprising even many decades later.

Apart from commemorating the Warsaw Uprising, another step was made to dedicate to commemorating the history of the Jewish community. In 2005, the foundation committee for the Jewish History Museum was established under president Aleksander Kwaśniewski (who was the second president of the Republic of Poland from 1995 to 2005, who replaced Lech Wałęsa). In 2007, the founding ceremony took place with Lech Kaczyński as the new president. Kaczyński was also supportive of the idea. After he died in the Smoleńsk airplane crash in 2010, former Warsaw insurgents, the Home Army veterans, and Warsaw Rising Museum staff decided to fund a plaque commemorating the former president of Poland and mayor of Warsaw [Fig.2-29].

Fig.2-29 A plaque dedicated to Lech Kaczyński, mayor of Warsaw in 2001-2005 and subsequent president of Poland in 2005-2010.

Now, it is important to take a glimpse of how the two museums were constructed, first discussing the Warsaw Rising Museum which was finished earlier. Located at the former Tram Electricity Power Station, the museum retained features of the original building. The tower of the Museum was decorated by using the Fighting Poland anchor symbol [Fig.2-30]. Inside, the exhibition is divided into several segments. One is dedicated to the little insurgents, of how the youngest of the insurgents were involved. Some exhibitions describe the Uprising day by day (from 1st August till 2nd October 1944). In addition, the museum added elements for visitors to help them understand better the reality of the Uprising and its aftermath of it. This included, apart from main artifacts of a period (weaponry, letters, documents concerning organization of the Polish Underground State), a copy of sewage canals which the insurgents used to move around the city. Later on, a short film projection entitled *The City of Ruins* (2010) was added, which showed the post-uprising destruction of Warsaw. Finally, two exhibitions of the Museum consider the problems of Nazi Germany and the Soviet Union respectively. As for the Hitler Reich, it considers war crimes committed by the occupants and the military plans of the Wehrmacht to suppress the Uprising. When it comes to the Soviet Union, it shows the politics of Stalin towards the Warsaw Uprising and the fate of the insurgents after 1945. Outside of the main exhibition, several features were added to the Museum. These included replicas of some of the vehicles used during the Rising, the wall of the insurgents with all their names included, and the site for the popular art. Today, the Warsaw Rising Museum is the most well-known institutionalized place of memory about the Warsaw Uprising.

Fig.2-30 Warsaw Rising Museum, the main square. The tower visible in the rear features the "Fighting Poland" anchor—the symbol of World War II resistance.

Apart from the new museum, former sites of memory concerning the Uprising got their second life, Warsaw Insurgents Cemetery being a notable example. The first deceased was buried here in late 1945 and in 1946, the major mound was constructed. However, due to the political climate of the era, the cemetery project was not completed, making the necropolis unknown to most people. In the 1960s, the first headstones were placed at the necropolis, featuring the Grunwald Cross—a symbol very important for the narrative of the Polish People's Republic. In the 1970s, the Fallen-Unconquerable Monument (Polegli-Niepokonani) was unveiled. Having resemblance in form and message to Warsaw Heroes Monument, this site of memory did not originally specify commemoration of the Warsaw Uprising, but it paid the tribute to all the victims—Warsaw defense participants, two uprisings casualties, or those who were killed during the Nazi occupation in general. This changed in the early 2000s, when the monument was renovated. "Fighting Poland" anchor was added to his shield and new plaques were added describing the site [Fig.2-31]. In 2012, the necropolis was once again renovated. In a way, the history of this particular cemetery mirrors shifting narratives towards the Warsaw experience of the war—the 1944 Uprising in particular.

Fig.2-31 The Fallen-Unconquerable Monument. The monument depicts a fallen warrior carrying a giant shield. The statue is placed on the ground where ashes of 50,000 insugents were buried.

Some places of memory were readapted for newer times. During the final days of the Uprising, an artist Jan Małeta made the plaque "Christ, save us because we are dying" (*Jezu, ratuj, bo giniemy*). After World War II, the plaque was removed from the original site—the work by Karol Tchorek was placed instead. In 2013 a replica of the original Małeta's plaque was unveiled next to Tchorek's work. Both commemorations coexist with each other. Małeta's reconstructed sculpture makes a clear reference to the Polish martyrology, whereas Tchorek's plaques is more connected to the narrative of the Polish People's Republic [Fig.2-32].

Apart from bringing back to life former commemorations, other strategies included marking places that no longer existed in their original form. A good example of such a tendency is concerning the Warsaw Ghetto. Apart from erecting a monument that described in detail the former Ghetto, an effort was made to mark the former Ghetto walls [Fig.2-33]. By doing so, the visitors could rediscover the Jewish Ghetto and the community which was lost after World War II.

Fig.2-32 Karol Tchorek's plaque (center) together with the plaque "Christ, save us because we are dying" (right). Located at the Jerusalem Alleys (Aleje Jerozolimskie), No. 37 in Warsaw.

Fig.2-33 The monument commemorating the walls of the Warsaw Ghetto. The section is located on Chłodna Street.

Speaking of memorization of the Jewish community, the period of the 2000s and 2010s had many new projects. Apart from commemorating Warsaw Ghetto Uprising, there were attempts to honor individuals. One example could be featuring those who dedicated their work to help those the most needed.

In 2006, a monument was erected in memory of Janusz Korczak [Fig.2-34]. Korczak was a famous children pedagogue who run an orphanage in a Ghetto. When he was offered by "Żegota", the Council to Aid Jews, to leave the Ghetto, he refused it on the grounds that he would have to leave his pupils. Instead, on 5th or 6th August 1942, Korczak was sent together with children from his orphanage to Treblinka Death Camp.

Fig.2-34 Janusz Korczak Memorial. The statue is located at a site of the former Jewish orphanage. Today, the memorial lies in the vicinity of the Palace of Culture and Science.

Korczak was well known before the 2000s. His works were reprinted and translated to other languages, including *King Matty the First* (*Król Macius̀ Pierwszy*) and others. In 1990, Andrzej Wajda made a film *Korczak* about the "Old Doctor" (one of Korczak's pseudonyms). Even earlier in 1980, a cenotaph was made in the name of his memory. What made the new monument special was that it was unveiled during the new era of reexamining the past. Therefore, some of the heroes were once again commemorated, but some experienced greater admiration for the first time.

This happened to Irena Sendler, the pre-war Polish Socialist Party member and one of the most prominent figures of the Żegota. After the war, her undertakings were awarded in Poland as well as in Israel (she was declared Righteous Among Nations in 1965). She was rediscovered in the 2000s, being nominated twice for the Nobel Peace Prize. After she died in 2008, the memorization continued. In 2013, the pathway to the completed POLIN Museum of the History of Polish Jews was named after her.

A similar commemoration was delivered to Jan Karski, a courier and emissary of the Polish Underground State, who delivered in 1942-1943 an extensive statement on mass exterminations of the Jews. After the 2000s, one of the most common ways of commemoration was the Benches of Karski. The first one was unveiled in 2002 at George Washington University where he was a lecturer. In 2013, a similar bench was placed in Warsaw [Fig.2-35].

Fig.2-35 The Bench of Jan Karski. The statue is one of the examples commemorating a particular individual. It is also linked with the Holocaust narrative via the person of Jan Karski.

The Bench of Jan Karski was placed next to the POLIN Museum of the History of Polish Jews, which was finally opened in 2013 [Fig.2-36]. Unlike other commemorations, the POLIN Museum adopted a holistic approach towards Jewish history, from the beginning till the end. In doing so, it provides a full depiction of the Jewish community, its origins in the Middle Ages, its Renaissance in the Early Modern Period, its persecutions and national debates over identity in the 19th century, its vibrant life during the interwar period, the catastrophe of the Holocaust, the post-war situation, the 1968 March Events and the revival of the community after 1989. The opening of the POLIN Museum marked the 70th anniversary of the Warsaw Ghetto Uprising.

Meanwhile, the 70th anniversary of the Warsaw Uprising in 2014 marked the start of a new stage in memorization and narrative building in Warsaw and Poland. Since I view the current stage as not finished, I decided to end the discussion on memorization in this place. However, there are several points that I think are worthy to be observed in the next era.

First is the problem of the generation transition. Poland and Warsaw are slowly approaching the moment of lack of witness to past events. Probably the last insurgent of the Warsaw Ghetto Uprising Simcha Rotem passed away in December 2018. By 2014, the estimated number of living Warsaw Uprising insurgents was about 28,000 combatants. Assuming there are usually people who were born between the 1910s and the 1930s, by the year 2020, this gives an age between 80 and 100 years old. As the witnesses pass away, the younger generations lose the memory continuity.

Fig.2-36 The POLIN Museum of the History of Polish Jews. Together with memorials discussed earlier, the Museum is also involved in commemorating the Jewish community in Warsaw.

Fig.2-37 An example of street art connected with the Warsaw Uprising. Resistance soldiers are depicted next to inscriptions: "Warsaw Uprising, Wola (district) '44."

The communicative memory slowly transforms into the cultural one. Past events slowly move into the dimension of history and popular culture. The subject of the Rising can be seen in local street art [Fig.2-37]. This is just a small example illustrating the larger problem. How is the Warsaw Uprising, and Warsaw experience of World War II presented in popular literature, film, video games, and other media? Such a transition raises questions on the future commemoration of the wartime past, both in form and practice.

Another problem is the question of past memorization. Any memorization of the past is the byproduct of its times, thus later on it has to be altered. Monument to Brotherhood of Arms, which was mentioned early in the chapter as an example of early memorization of the War, was dismantled in 2011. In 2016, the Polish parliament passed legislation concerning banning communist symbols in public space. This sparked the debates over the interpretation of the new law, for instance, to what extent is People's Army Alley just a commemoration of Partisans or an embodiment of the former political system? The legacy of the Polish People's Republic period reflects problems for the narrative. The very important issue is, to what extent the former narratives could be useful for contemporary purposes.

The formation of collective memory and historical narrative is also a multi-dimensional process. As a result, the newest trends cannot be fully discussed and the analysis needs to end here. The end of the 2004-2014 decade in remembering marked the 70th anniversary of the Uprising. Since the 70th anniversary in 2014, new tendencies emerge, yet it is still uncertain how they are going to develop.

For the sake of consistency of the book, I decide to end up here describing the postwar memory changes and the historical narrative building. The purpose here is not to study the narrative itself. Rather, I attempt to place the collective memory changes and narrative building in the greater context. The knowledge we presented in this chapter would be useful, as collective memory and narrative building shaped the post-war conditions for peace and reconciliation in Warsaw.

Chapter 3

Peace and Reconciliation Process: Warsaw Peacebuilding and the Polish-German Dialogue

The reader might have noticed a problem within Chapter Two. We focused mostly on discussion among different Poland-based social actors (the government, the insurgents, the later generations, the Jewish community). The discussion mostly focused on memory and historical narrative. However, discussions concerning the past were also aimed at reconciling with it. Furthermore, reconciling with one's past is also connected with "the other". In other words, where Warsaw was a victim, there was a perpetrator too, and that perpetrator was Nazi Germany. Therefore, in the final Chapter of the book, I am going to discuss how broader peacebuilding occurred in Warsaw and how the city played a vital role in reconciling with "the other". But before that, let us outline the most important terms for this part, including the concept of peace itself.

Concepts of Peace, Studies of Peace and Reconciliation

Discussions about peace existed since the beginning. In the West, the concept of peace and its meaning were debated by many generations of thinkers. These included philosophers of Ancient Greece (primarily Aristotle), medieval theologians (e.g. sir Thomas Aquinas) as well as Early Modern and Modern thinkers (John Locke, Immanuel Kant, Jean Jacques Rousseau). Ideas of peace existed in other traditions as well, including Islam, Buddhism, Confucianism, etc.

Nevertheless, for a long time, there was no formalized research on peace or social activism for peace. Part of the reason was that war before the 19th century was considered to be a natural element of politics. To quote 19th-century military strategist Carl von Clausewitz: "War is not merely a political act, but also a real political instrument, a continuation of political commerce, a carrying out of the same by other means."

The attitude towards war gradually changed as the means of conducting it became more and more brutal. In these new circumstances, war was not just merely a fight between two armies, but meant larger destruction of entire cities and communities as well as the suffering of civilians. Such a development partially influenced the rise of institutionalized peace activism at the turn from the 19th to the 20th century. The final influence came from World War I and World War II. Both World Wars of the 20th century successfully undermined the past idea of a "just war". This, as well as the fear of another World War, accelerated further developments in peace activism as well as the rise of academic studies regarding peace.

Several terms denote the kind of academic research whose subject is peace. A reader may find it under the term "peace research", "peace studies", "peace and conflict studies" or even "irenology". Sometimes these terms are synonyms, sometimes they point out different tendencies within the same field of studies. For the sake of clarity, we treat all the terms synonymously. All of them denote a social science that has a multidisciplinary character. Peace studies combine knowledge taken from sociology, anthropology, psychology, international relations, political sciences, and many more. It aims to analyze violent and non-violent behaviors to promote peace. Theories of peace were developed by academics such as Johan Galtung. Peace agendas are currently proposed by international organizations such as the United Nations.

The Polish experience concerning peace research generally followed world tendencies, especially those of Europe. Poland's understanding of the notion became heavily influenced by Christian thought after it became the dominant religion in the Middle Ages. The Late Medieval Polish theologian Paweł Włodkowic elaborated on the distinction between just and unjust wars. He perceived peace as a right given by God for people regardless of their religions. In the eyes of God, all people are made brethren, whether they are Christian or not, and all people should be loved. "So, if the non-believers want to live in peace among Christians, then one shall not hurt them or their property." This thinking carried on throughout the centuries. Polish nobles enacted in 1573 the earlier mentioned Warsaw Confederation, an act which guaranteed religious tolerance. As in Europe, in Poland, another source of interpretation for peace emerged which came from people of more secular background. Polish king and statesman Stanisław Leszczyński made remarks on peace during the Age of Enlightenment in his philosophical treaty *Idea Wiecznego Pokoju* (*On Idea of Perpetual Peace*). Poles also took part in emerging peace activism in the 19th century and later on during World War I, the interwar period, and after World War II. Many times they were associated with international organizations such as the League of Nations and the UN. Thus peace category was also used in a political context, and this aspect will be presented in the book about the reconciliation process which happened after World War II.

Apart from peace activism, peace research also started to emerge as a constituent social science in Poland. Some of the people involved in the process we're discussing it from the standpoint of Christianity. The other direction went to discuss peace in categories of national and international safety, peace education, and peace culture. Thus peace studies were put in international relations framework or being followed by "sister" science called the war studies or polemology. In Poland, peace research is called "irenologia" (irenology), "badania nad pokojem" (peace research) and "nauka o pokoju" (peace studies).

Now, after describing the peace-related activities, we may go back to the original question—how to understand "peace"? We may consider a definition proposed by the authors of *Handbook of Peace Studies*. In the publication, Charles Webel and Johan Galtung distinguished "positive" and "negative" peace. "Positive" peace denotes the simultaneous presence of many desirable states of mind and society, such as harmony, justice, equity, etc. "Negative" peace has historically denoted the "absence of war and other forms of widescale violent human conflict." Similar to "peace" category, the authors of the *Handbook* propose a dual understanding of the term "peace culture". Defined as the "absence of cultural violence", the peace culture in its negative sense could mean overcoming different prejudices. The prejudices can be based on different aspects, including nationality, age, race, class, religion, and more. The "negative" peace culture also means "elimination of the glorification of war and violence in the media, literature, films, monuments, etc.". In the positive sense of the word, the peace culture includes "promotion of a culture of peace and mutual learning", "global communication and dialogues" and many more.

Thus "peace" and "peace culture" describe a particular state, but what describes an action for peace? Here, we may consider using the term peacebuilding. It was characterized by former General Secretary of the UN Boutros Boutros-Ghali in his *An Agenda For Peace* as "finding means of strengthening peace and avoiding conflict". The authors of the *Handbook* described peacebuilding in further detail. What becomes necessary for peacebuilding "is the civil disobedience of establishing contact with the appointed enemy, engaging in positive, helpful, cooperative relations instead". Actors engaged in peacebuilding refuse "to structure the inner world in that polarized way, also identifying the negative in Self and the positive in Other". That is not to say that we should only see the negatives in ourselves and only see positives in other. "Avoiding the trap of Self-hatred combined with Other-love; that is only polarization in reverse, not reversed."

Naturally, we do not necessarily have to describe all of our actions as "peacebuilding". In the case of Warsaw and Polish-German relations, various initiatives were described with other names, including the term "reconciliation". Authors of the *Handbook* define it as "a state of peace to the relationship, where the entities are at least not harming each other". Joanna Santa-Barbara added that the "revenge is foregone as an option": parties involved in reconciliation trust one another that harming will not appear. Here, any reconciliation is related to the notion of forgiveness: "Forgiveness means that the moral debt is canceled; anger and resentment are dropped; there will be no revenge."

Naturally, the concept of peace is far from being only an abstract term debated by scholars. For those affected by the war or other conflict, living a peaceful life afterward is a more down-to-earth problem. Similarly, for many of Warsaw inhabitants who went through the horrors of World War II, life after the War was not about an academic debate over memory or peacebuilding or another idea, but rather urgent needs: how to rebuild one's home and one's city, how to cope with the trauma caused by the conflict. Then, this trauma was not just a matter of a single person in Warsaw; it was shared with other dwellers and consequently, linked with the former perpetrators. Finding peace in Warsaw was a matter of the Polish-German Reconciliation.

This is why I often combine the two concepts into one: peace and reconciliation. If peacebuilding is about "finding means of strengthening peace and avoiding conflict", then reconciliation can be seen as a process linked with peacebuilding, but still autonomous. We are going to examine a specific example, namely, the postwar peace and reconciliation process between Poland and Germany and the role of Warsaw in that process. We would try to examine, how two nations built their respective narratives on the past, engaged in telling the story to one another and thus enabling the mutual reconciliation.

After Chapter Two, we grasped how Warsaw experience of the war was being remembered, and based on this memory, what narratives were constructed. But how did these narratives influence the Warsaw peacebuilding and the Polish-German reconciliation? What was special for the peace and reconciliation process that occurred in Warsaw? And, why such an experience might be important for broader communities: not just Warsaw local or Polish national, but for the international ones too?

Between the "Fighting for Peace" and the Reckoning with the Past

When the War ended in 1945, the Poles and the Germans had to face a new reality. As a result of the Allied Conferences of Tehran, Yalta, and Potsdam, the Polish borders were moved to the West. Poland received the territories which belonged formerly to Germany. Cities of Breslau or Danzig were renamed as Wrocław and Gdańsk. At the same time, Poland lost its territories to the East. The territorial changes were followed by forced resettlements. Poles and Germans had to leave their former homes because their countries' borders shifted one way or another. To make the matter even more complicated, one Polish state had to engage with two Germanies: the Federal Republic of Germany (or West Germany) which was integrated with the Western political structures, and East Germany, officially known as the German Democratic Republic, became an important member of the Eastern Bloc.

It is not the role of this book to discuss geopolitics. However, the geopolitical situation of Poland affected how the peace problem was treated in the country. The war against Germany was interpreted not just as a national struggle, but (foremost) as the ideological one. It was the struggle against fascism, the struggle which was eventually won by the Allies. However, the official narrative in postwar Poland identified a new threat to world peace: the United States and Western Imperialism. The official narrative described peace as something endangered, something which one had to actively struggle for. The narrative encouraged people and governments to mobilize to the threats for peace, even enemies of peace.

I refer to such rhetoric which occurred in post-war Poland as the "fighting for peace" (pol. walka o pokój) narrative. It was violent in a sense. "The threat" or "the enemy" was not something or somebody one could have a dialogue with. The only option was to fight with the threat or with the enemy.

In 1948, the World Congress of Intellectuals in Defense of Peace was held in the city of Wrocław, Poland. The choice of Wrocław was deliberate: formerly belonging to Germany before World War II, the city was ceded to Poland after 1945. Officially though, Wrocław represented "the recovered territories" (pol. ziemie odzyskane). According to the narrative, they were formerly part of the Polish state, now reclaimed after thousands of years. The original Polish Duchy, whose ruler Mieszko I from the Piast dynasty converted to Christianity in 966, had its borders on the Oder-Nysse Line. Now, almost one millennium later, the new post-war Polish government reclaimed lands of the Piast state—from the Germans. When the World Congress of Intellectuals in Defense of Peace was held, another event simultaneously took place: The Exhibition of Recovered Territories.

Still, the World Congress of Intellectuals in Defense of Peace received considerable interest. Delegates included the UNESCO director Julian Huxley, French physicist Irene Joliot-Curie, Polish poet Jarosław Iwaszkiewicz, German writer Anna Seghers and many others. Despite promoting an agenda for peace, the World Congress also became an element of cold-war politics. The Soviet Union delegates focused heavily on the threat coming from the "American Imperialism" and on critique towards Western intellectuals. Delegates from Western countries (notably France, the UK, and the US) were outraged by the rhetoric and presented their objections. Some delegates tried a more conciliatory approach. The dove of peace was proposed during that Congress by Pablo Picasso as a symbol of the entire movement.

The Congress in Wroclaw paved the way for similar initiatives later on. In November 1950, the World Congress of the Supporters of Peace was held in Warsaw [Fig.3-1]. The event was organized after the cancellation of the originally planned congress in Sheffield in the United Kingdom. After the event, the organizers published a multi-language brochure. On one hand, it stressed Warsaw being a meaningful place to organize the Congress. "Warsaw… one of the cities most destroyed by the war, by Nazi fascism." Thus the organizers linked the Warsaw experience with the idea of promoting peace. On the other hand, the brochure in general repeated the "fighting for peace" narrative. The "fight for peace" was not for reconciling with the other, rather, it was aimed at the new Other.

For further reference, we may look at the brochure from the 1950s "We are fighting for peace in the world" (*Walczymy o pokój na świecie*). The Central Committee of the Physical Culture (Główny Komitet Kultury Fizycznej), who published the brochure as a collective work, was an governmental agency. Throughout its existence under different names, the Committee co-organized sports events which promoted the official narrative—including the "fighting for peace" rhetoric. One of examples of it was the Peace Race (pol. Wyścig pokoju), a cycling sports competition organized annually.

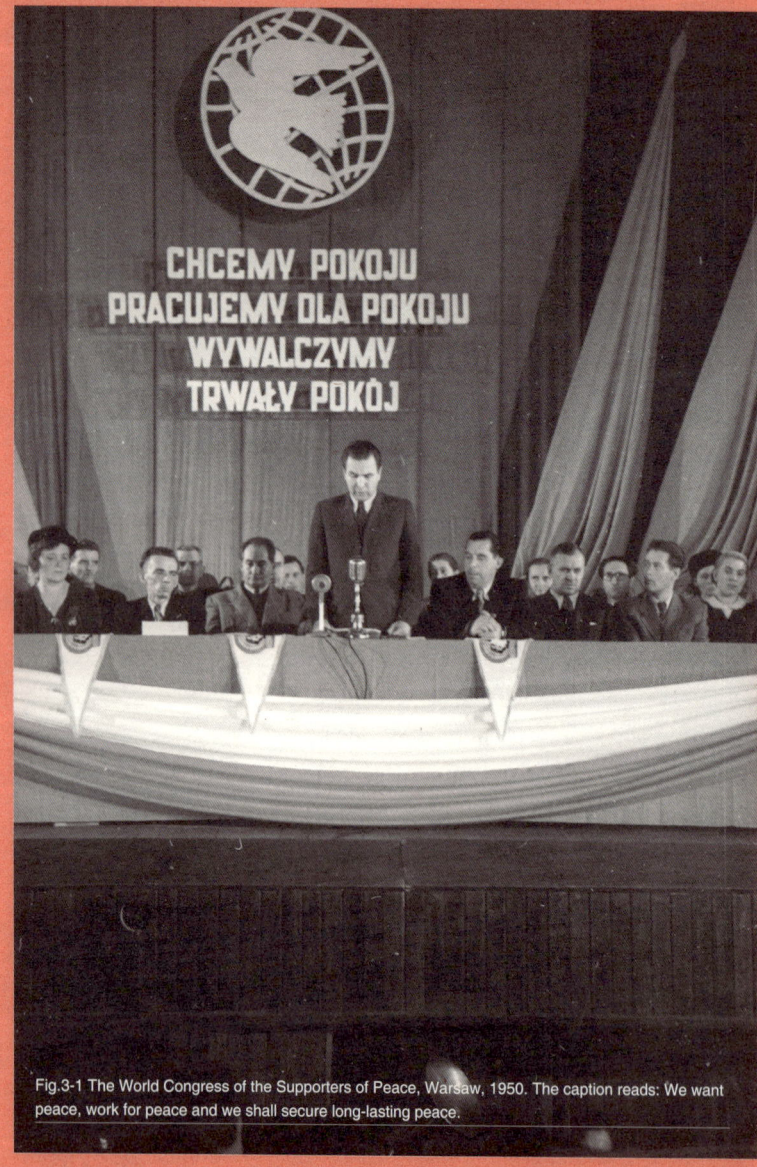

Fig.3-1 The World Congress of the Supporters of Peace, Warsaw, 1950. The caption reads: We want peace, work for peace and we shall secure long-lasting peace.

The content of this publication compiled by the Committee is a good example of the peace narrative during that era. The authors asserted that the source of war came from a desire for profit from capitalist and imperialist countries. When it comes to Germany, the brochure drew a sharp distinction. East Germany was perceived as the one which sought peace with Poland. The other, West Germany, was presented as an asylum of Hitlerism and a base for American Imperialism, a potential enemy which did not accept the new Polish-German border. The argument hardly could be ignored. The border change after World War II was also a tragedy for the Germans. People who lived in places such as Wroclaw/Breslau before the War had to move to a place that was their country, but not their original home. The West German society was not keen at that time to accept the new border between the two states. Meanwhile, in Poland, an alliance with the Eastern Bloc could be seen as a guarantee that the Polish-German frontier would be respected. However, such conditions naturally prevented any possibility for peace and reconciliation with the West German counterpart.

For now, Poland came to terms with the newly formed German Democratic Republic. Its existence forced a change in the historical narrative considering the War. When we look at monuments erected before 1949 considering World War II, they specifically referred to the former perpetrator as "the Germans". After 1949, memorization sites in Poland started to use the term "Hitlerites" and "fascists"—this was to avoid targeting East Germany and to point out West Germany as the main perpetrator. However, as Jerzy Wiatr noted, "such change of language had positive consequences. It was the first step toward overcoming the climate of hostility toward all Germans".

Officially, the relations between Polish People's Republic and the German Democratic Republic were presented by the government as an example of good relations. In 1950, two governments met at Zgorzelec/Görlitz to sign a treaty of border and friendship. It specified borders between Poland and East Germany on the Oder-Nysse Line. However, any further reconciliation attempts on the governmental level were limited. Part of the problem lied in the "anti-fascist" narrative adopted by the GDR. According to this narrative, East Germany was a worker-peasant state and an embodiment of the anti-fascist tendencies of the two classes: workers and peasants. Being conscious that their interests are contradictory towards the interests of capitalists, rejected systems that were supportive of the ruling class: fascism and liberal capitalist democracy. However, the narrative was not just a mere interpretation of Marxist thought for the East German government. As Kazimierz Wóycicki noted, "it was a particular answer towards the specific problems of the German identity".

Same as Western counterparts, the East Germans faced the problem of attitude towards the past. How to deal with the Nazi period? What was the guilt of the German people? The East German dominant narrative dealt with these topics. According to the narrative, Germany previously experienced failed revolutions: the German Peasant War of 1525, the Spring of Nations of 1848, and the Spartacist Uprising of 1918. All of them succumbed to the forces of capitalism and fascism. Here, fascism was perceived as a by-product of capitalism, a result of a historic necessity rather than something peculiar to the German nation. Thus the blame and responsibility for the rise of fascism could not be put entirely on Germany. Within this narrative, the Germans could feel liberated from the guilt. Moreover, since the narrative disconnected fascism from the national element, the Germans could have seen themselves as its first victims. The Nazi period was viewed as a liberation from fascism rather than a time to reflect upon it.

Such a narrative influenced the attitude towards the former National Socialist German Workers Party (National socialistische Deutsche Arbeiterpartei, NSDAP). On one hand, the leaders of the Nazi Party who were considered to be guilty would be executed early on after the War ended. On the other hand, the new Socialist Unity Party of Germany (Sozialistische Einheitspartei Deutschlands, SED) admitted former Nazi Party members provided they were "passive members" and without guilt. What was more important for Polish-German relations was that the East German attitude disabled a deeper reflection towards the past. The national blame for the emergence of Hitler could be pushed back, moreover, could be passed on the West Germans even though the leader of the Third Reich did not originate from that region.

The East German official narrative, therefore, interpreted the end of World War II not necessarily as Germany's defeat, but rather as liberation from fascism. The creation of the GDR was perceived as a part of that liberation. Kazimierz Wóycicki observed that in this narrative, "Since fascism was a product of capitalist relations, regime change itself was the most effective, indeed the only radically effective, means of anti-fascist therapy". Thus, there was little motivation left in circles related to the GDR government to engage in a dialogue about the past, also about the past of Polish-German relations.

In terms of post-war reconciliation, the role of East Germany was gradually overshadowed by its stronger Western counterpart. Due to its political and economic power, the Federal Republic had the stronger mandate to represent the entire German nation in future talks about reconciliation. However, another factor that explained the West German role in the reconciliation was the emerging debate about the past.

The discussion in West Germany was influenced by the program of implemented denazification by the Allies. It was part of the "reckoning with the past" as scholars referred to it. As Kazimierz Wóycicki noted in his book *Niemiecki rachunek Sumienia* (*German Account of Conscience*), " 'The reckoning' was imposed on the Germans after World War II" by the Allies. But, "as the time passed, the Germans took it as a responsibility". The Germans watched films such as *Windmills of death* (*Todesmühlen*, directed in 1945), which presented Nazi Concentration Camps, and schools had to teach about war crimes of Hitler. Apart from discovering the true horror of atrocities, such exposition shook the very notions of German society.

People discovered that the very same authority they obeyed was morally bankrupt. Thus it should not be surprising that the new West German elites ofttimes came from politicians who contested Nazi ideology at the time. The new chancellor Konrad Adenauer was once a member of the former Zentrum Party, a party which came into being before World War I. Adenauer and his associates managed to rally different Catholic and Protestant groups into one coherent political force: the Christian Democratic Union (Christlich-Demokratische Union, CDU). Chancellor's charisma, a desire for leadership in German society, and a wariness of West German society towards developments in Eastern Bloc which the CDU expressed stabilized the political situation within the new country. However, similarly to Poland, the West German political stance towards "the Other" (Poland, East Germany, the Eastern Bloc) meant that the reconciliation process could not advance further.

The discussion about the past was mostly limited to intellectuals and particular groups such as the former expelled. Intellectuals such as Karl Jaspers tried to frame the problem of German guilt in philosophical terms. His work resulted in conceptual framing why what happened during World War II was not only a problem for former leaders of Nazi Germany but also for the entire German society at the time. Jaspers' undertakings and later attempts by public intellectuals were linked with the "reckoning with the past". As Kazimierz Wóycicki noted that by rethinking the responsibility for the "bad past", "very thoroughly restructures the social image of the past". As the Germans gradually perceived the past in a different light and felt increasingly responsible for the Nazi period, the future reconciliation with the Polish counterpart could be possible.

Among interested groups, people expelled from the Eastern regions voiced their opinions during this period. On 5th August 1950, the Central Union of Germans Expellees along with United East German Landsmanshaft (type of mutual aid societies) signed the German Expellees from the Motherland Charter (Charta der Deutschen Heimatvertriebenen). What is interesting to note is that some elements of the charter were written in reconciling tone: "We, the expellees, resign from vengeance and retaliation. We treat this decision seriously and treat it as a holy one as it comes from memory about countless suffering that humanities had to face, especially in the last decade." As Kazimierz Wóycicki noted, the charter was far from being flawless. The phrase about the suffering of humanity, especially within the last decade, was vague and did not refer specifically to the suffering of particular nations. However, he noted that "renouncing vengeance was surely an act which required moral courage". It should be noted that the Expellees were a special group in this discussion. At the same time we could hear other voices in German public opinion. Attitudes presented included: denial of guilt ("Concentration camps were not invented by the Germans, but the British—after the Boer War in South Africa…"), displacement from memory ("We had no idea about that!") or relativization ("Hitler did not just do bad things, but he also did good ones, such as building highways"). The German public as a whole needed time for a deeper reflection. As Jerzy Wiatr remarked on first years of Polish German reconciliation: "On both sides, people tended to remember their own suffering and to ignore the suffering of the other nation. Emotional trauma was so great that only very few were able to look at the Polish-German relations from a longer historical perspective. The rethinking of the past was yet to come."

The Breakthrough in Peace and Reconciliation

The climate between Poland and Germany gradually changed after 1956. With the change in the leadership in the Eastern Bloc, the Polish government saw to improve relations with the Western countries. It was still far from reaching a breakthrough in reconciliation. However, as generations and the political climate changed, certain progress became possible. In Warsaw, the government and the former insurgents were slowly rethinking the memorization of the war. In West Germany, Chancellor Konrad Adenauer expressed his willingness to reconcile with Poland for the 20th anniversary of the War, but he never managed to do that, partially because it was too early for the main representative of the government to speak on behalf of the Germans. The move towards reconciliation was to come from Christian tradition on one side, and the generation change on the other.

In her study *Peace at all costs*, Annika Frieberg examined the role of Christian intellectuals for the Polish-German reconciliation. On German side, she categorized people involved in reconciliation into two groups. First, they were religious activists. For Catholics, the Bernsberger Circle stood out as a group which "wished to improve Polish-German relations and opposed West German nuclear rearmament". For Protestants, the East-German group Aktion Sühnezeichen "made efforts toward reconciliation through traveling to Poland, visiting concentration camps, and performing service there—demonstrations of penance on behalf of the German nation". Then, there was more loosely based group of "media personalities, reporters, and journalists working for elite journals and newspapers". These included: "The editor of *Die Zeit*, the Countess Marion Dönhoff, the editor of *Stern*, Henri Nannen, and the director general of WDR, Klaus von Bismarck, great nephew of Germany's 'Iron Chancellor' Otto von Bismarck and former Wehrmacht officer and Prussian landowner (…)."

On Polish side, Catholic intellectuals such as Jerzy Turowicz, Władysław Bartoszewski and Tadeusz Mazowiecki engaged in publishing journals. These included the *Tygodnik Powszechny* (Weekly Journal), *Więź* (The Bond) and *Znak* (Sign, Symbol)—all of them being semi-independent entities from the official press. The Catholic intelligentsia organized political representation too. After October Thaw in 1956, Władysław Gomułka along with other Polish communists held more tolerant views towards Catholic Church influence. In 1957, a group of MPs in the Polish Parliament established an informal "Znak" association. Its representatives such as Stanisław Stomma and Stefan Kisielewski hoped they could ameliorate the situation of Polish Catholics.

However, the "Znak" and other groups did not limit themselves to local situation. As Annika Frieberg noted: "Between the 1950s and the 1970s, these members of the Catholic intelligentsia and writers for the Catholic journals engaged with West German media personalities and travelers. Members of church hierarchy who supported the lay groups and, to an extent, the West German dialogue included Cardinal Karol Wojtyła of Cracow (later Pope John Paul II) as well as Bolesław Kominek, the archbishop of Wrocław." [Fig.3-2]

Fig.3-2 Archibishop Karol Wojtyła and future Pope John Paul II (left), archbishop Bolesław Kominek (center) and archbishop Antoni Baraniak (right) during celebrations of the Millennium of Poland's Christening in 1966.

As we can see, the Polish-German reconciliation involved many "civic society actors"—as Annika Frieberg described Christian-affiliated Church leaders and intellectuals. Thus peace and reconciliation process described here relied not just on outstanding intellectuals. It was also a collective effort of various groups. An eventual impulse for further actions of these groups came from Poland circumstances and from the Vatican.

In the early 1960s, the Polish Catholic Church prepared itself for celebration for the Poland's Millenium. In 966, Polish duke Mieszko I received baptism, thus bringing the young Polish state into a family of Chrisitan countries in Europe. Preparations for the millennial anniversary coincided with the proceedings of the Second Vatican Council. Held from 1962 to 1965, the Council became a cradle of reforms for the Catholic Church.

At the time of the Council, Christian circles in Germany made remarks concerning Polish-German Reconciliation. Several secular members of the evangelic Church, including mentioned earlier Klaus Bismarck signed the Tübingen Memorandum. The group called for reconsideration of West Germany towards the Eastern policy and declared their support for the Oder-Nysse border. In 1965, the Evangelical Church of Germany presented the memorial "On the situation of the expellees and the attitude of the German nation towards its Eastern neighbors". In Poland, the Catholic Church prepared for celebrations concerning the 1000th anniversary of Poland's baptism. For this occasion, the Catholic Church in Poland prepared invitation letters to Catholic hierarchs around the world. As Wojciech Kucharski noted in his compilation *Listy Millenijne* (Millenium Letters), the most influential of these documents was the one addressed to the German bishops. Presented as the "Pastoral Letter of the Polish Bishops to their German Brothers" (in Polish: Orędzie biskupów polskich do ich niemieckich braci w Chrystusowym urzędzie pasterskim; in German: Hirtenbrief der polnischen Bischöfe an ihre deutschen Amtsbrüder). Kucharski also remarked that researchers often overlooked how the letter actually came to being. For the letter to the "German brothers", the scholars agree that the Wrocław Archbishop Bolesław Kominek was the main author and compiler.

Apart from Archbishop Kominek, many prominent hierarchs of the Catholic Church in Poland signed the document. However, it was primarily the content of the letter that proved to be groundbreaking.

In the document, the Polish bishops specifically addressed present circumstances at the time and the troubling past. They opened the letter with an invitation to "German Brothers" to partake the celebrations of "the millennial anniversary of its baptism as well as 1,000 years of its national and state existence". Later on, the document mentioned many positive elements from common Polish-German history. The bishops stressed the common Christian culture which bound two countries together. However, they also mentioned more sorrowful part of history: clashes with the medieval Teutonic Knights and the Prussian Kingdom, the partitions of the 18th century, the suffering the Poles endured during the 150 years of existing as a nation without its state.

The Polish bishops continued their examination of the common past: "After a short, but lasting 20 years of independence (1918-1939), the Polish nation broke out something, which was called euphemistically World War II, but what was for us, Polish people, thought to be as an act of destruction and extermination." Despite being referred to as the "German occupation", Polish bishops described what weight this term bore. It meant the death of "6 million Polish citizens, mostly of Jewish origin", concentration camps, "from which crematoria chimneys smoked day and night", mass executions and many more. After the War, many of the Poles had to leave their homes due to changes in national borders. But, as Polish bishops commented: "Where were they (the Poles) supposed to go, anyway, when the so-called General Government together with the capital Warsaw lay in ruins." Despite that, the Polish bishops stressed the reason they described atrocities of World War II and postwar trauma was "only to make us more understandable today, both ourselves and our way of thinking today".

At the same time, the bishops acknowledged the sorrows of the German nation—those who were expelled from their homeland, the change of the Polish-German border. This was to do not paint a one-sided image of Germans, as they also experienced being a victim and being resistant—the White Rose Movement being a notable example. The bishops also emphasized on some of the common experiences in the suffering: "Thousands of Germans, both Christians, and communists, shared in our concentration camps the fate of our Polish brothers."

Here, an examination of mutual history ultimately led Polish bishops to the following conclusion: an appeal for reconciliation:

> *And despite all of that, despite this situation which hopelessly wears a burden of the past, in this situation we call you Dear Brothers: let us try to forget. No arguments, no further cold war, but the start of the dialogue(…) if on both sides there will be goodwill—and presumably we don't have to doubt it—a serious dialogue must succeed and will bring good fruit despite all of this, despite the "heated iron"(…) In this Christian, but also very human spirit, we offer our hands to you who are sitting on benches of the Council about to end, we present forgiveness and we ask you for the same.*

What was groundbreaking was not only the matter of simply calling for forgiveness. Archbishop Kominek and other signatories of the letter [Fig.3-3] addressed two sources of the conflict: the one linked with the past and with the present (that is, at the time of writing this letter).

As far as the past was concerned, the bishops discussed events that happened and that were remembered: We might recall Warsaw Heroes Monument constructed in the 1960s. The monument's main figure is Nike: goddess of victory. She holds a giant Grunwald sword—a clear reference to the Grunwald Battle of 1410 when the Polish-Lithuanian army defeated the Teutonic Knights forces. The cultural memory about the battle, as well as later events: the Prussian rise to power, the partitions of the 18th century, the assimilation policies targeting Polish people: all were part of the national narrative at that time. Even though these events were largely bygone, they nevertheless mastered, primarily because they were linked with more recent atrocities of World War II. The trauma about "the final catastrophe prepared by Hitler" was very fresh.

Fig.3-3 Pastoral Letter of the Polish Bishops to their German Brothers. The front page indicated that the letter was thought of as an invitation for the Millenial Celebration of Poland's baptism.

Speaking of contemporary times, the letter addressed the problem of the Polish-German border, the fear of a renewed conflict between the nations. But, signatories of the letter stressed that the answer should not be vengeance. Rather, the function of restating past events was to comprehend one's background, in this case, being contemporary Polish people. Moreover, the bishops continued with considering the standpoint of the German counterpart. The proposal for ending the hostility were these words: "We present forgiveness and we ask you for the same."

This statement exceeded the circumstances of the era. Sylwia Dec-Pustelnik characterized the response of the German bishops as "rather restraint". Even though they welcomed the invitation for attending the Millenial celebrations, the German bishops' response "lacked unequivocal declarations, which could lead to overcoming barriers in mutual contacts". The government back in Poland was infuriated by the initiative. It blamed Catholic bishops for not representing the interests of the country. Many contemporary Poles opposed the content of the letter. They were dissatisfied with mentioning the "Polish sins".

Nevertheless, it was with later generations that the document became recognized as one of many important milestones in Polish-German reconciliation. From the present, we may observe that the letter had its peace-building role: it promoted mutual understanding, renouncing violence and vengeance. Despite heavy criticism, the bishops did not perpetuate "We vs. the Other", but rather went one step further to reconcile with the Other.

The next change came from the generational change and developments in West Germany. Kazimierz Wóycicki remarked that "the German conscience started to awake". For him, there were several reasons for the awakening. New memoirs and literature about the war, including diaries of Anne Frank published in 1957, and Gunther Grass' *The Tin Drum* (*Die Blechtrommel*) posed new questions and new facts about the war. New historical research deepened the knowledge about the Nazi period, for instance in Karl Dietrich Bracher's *Downfall of the Weimar Republic* (*Auflössung der Weimar Republik*). Some historians went further by questioning the traditional German historiography. Newer researchers such as Fritz Fischer showed that the Nazi period was not an accident, but rather a development of earlier tendencies existing in Imperial Germany before World War I.

Contemporary events played their role as well. The Krushchev Thaw of 1956 contributed to the weakening of the anti-communist rhetoric within West Germany. In 1961, the Israeli authorities conducted a trial of Adolf Eichman, one of the main organizers of the "Final Solution of the Jewish Question". The trial, which ended with the death penalty of Eichmann, influenced the later stance of the German government and the public opinion. People were more inclined to believe that crimes conducted during World War II should not expire.

An overall generational transition was also influential. The generation of war witnesses was already middle-aged or elderly. For them, they either preferred to remain silent about the past or to find the strategy to erase the sense of guilt. Their children, the so-called "skeptical generation", were people who experienced the War as teenagers. The experience caused them to be distrustful towards public life. Compared with their parents, they felt ashamed of the past events, but they could not describe the sources of guilt. Compared to "the skeptics", the third generation was ready to openly rebel against the Nazi past. Born after the War, "the rebels" largely influenced West German politics of the 1960s and 1970s.

These tendencies helped the Social Democratic Party (the SPD) engage in the reconciliation process. In 1958, Carlo Schmid visited Warsaw, where he visited the Ghetto Heroes Monument and the Pawiak Prison. In a commemorative book, he wrote the following statement: "Being deeply ashamed in this place of disgrace, hoping for the hope for humanity." However, the SPD at the time was an opposition party. It was not until 1969 that it won the elections in West Germany.

The new chancellor Willy Brandt called for the "new eastern policy" (Neue Ostpolitik). The main goal of it was a gradual rapprochement with East Germany, the USSR, Poland and other countries with the Eastern Bloc. However, it was not simply a diplomatic policy: Ospolitik did have peacebuilding and reconciliation undertones. As it was put by Martin Brochet, who was an influential historian within the SPD ranks: "There, where history led to a catastrophe, it is a necessity and a daring need to rethink self-critically its ways (that is, ways of history). It is especially important for our attitude towards the Polish nation." Later in 1972, he added that the debate over history "must reach deeper to the times before Hitler, and it must cover the past relations with Eastern Europe and even older origins of poisoning relations with the Polish nation".

On Polish side, members of the Znak Circle such as Stanisław Stomma proved to be once again important in fostering the mutual dialogue. However, there was one remaining actor which was affiliated with the government. As Jerzy Wiatr described it, when the Catholic Press such as Tygodnik Powszechny voiced out arguments for mutual reconciliation and peace, "similar arguments one could find on the pages of the weekly 'Polityka', the unofficial organ of the liberal wing of the Polish United Workers Party". Among the "Polityka" journalists was Mieczysław Rakowski. Rakowski completed his PhD thesis regarding the history of the German SPD. Later on, he established contacts with influential social democrats in Germany, including Egon Bahr—one of the primary architects of the Ostpolitik.

In 1970, Brandt started visiting countries within the Eastern Bloc. In August, he arrived in the Soviet Union, where he and Brezhnev agreed on the new Polish-German border. However, the First Secretary of the PUWP Władysław Gomułka did not trust this agreement as it reminded him of gloomy past of Poland's powerful neighbors talking behind its back. Thus Poland and West Germany negotiated separate treaty. After successful negotiations, the Polish counterparts invited the West German delegation to visit Warsaw. On 6th December 1970, Willy Brandt signd the new border treaty.

The first moments of the visit proved to be difficult for both sides. Brandt was greeted by prime minister Józef Cyrankiewicz, a former prisoner of Auschwitz Concentration Camp. After the greeting, Brandt received a welcome from the Representative Honor Guards of the Polish Armed forces. The company started to play the National Anthem of Germany for the first time since the ending of the War. Mieczysław Rakowski felt that something "squeezed his throat", Brandt was also touched as tears were dripping on his face. The very same day, a small banquet was hosted by Władysław Gomułka for the German guests. Despite a tense atmosphere in the beginning, the dinner helped to cool down tensions between the two sides. On next day, the Warsaw Treaty was signed by the two parties.

Later during the day, Brandt visited the Monument of the Unknown Soldier, a traditional site of memory dedicated to Polish veterans fallen for the Homeland. As it was the standard ritual for all leaders—Brandt was to pay the tribute by bowing and presenting flowers from the German delegation. However, the Germans asked the Polish side to allow them to visit another site of memory—the Warsaw Ghetto Heroes Monument. The Polish Government agreed, however, it insisted that the visit to the memorial should be less official, for instance, without the assistance of the representation company.

Before noon, Brandt, along with politicians and journalists arrived near the Ghetto Heroes Monument. After laying down a wreath, Brandt, all of a sudden, knelt, to the big surprise of the audience. Then, he remained so for half a minute [Fig.3-4]. No one said anything, the perfect silence was sometimes disturbed by the falling snow. After the gesture, Brandt stood up with a solemn face. One of journalists commented on the situation: "Then he knelt, he who has no need to, on behalf of all who ought to kneel but don't – because they dare not, or cannot venture to do so."

Fig.3-4 Willy Brandt's Kniefall—kneeling in front of the Ghetto Heroes Monument. The photo became a universally recognizable symbol for the Polish-German reconciliation.

The commentary was a very insightful one. Brandt, a social-democrat, who escaped Germany before the Nazi takeover to avoid further persecutions, made a gesture on behalf of those who were not willing to do it. People who witnessed or who were immediately informed about the situation were deeply moved. In a more popular article about the event, Polish journalist Arkadiusz Stempin quoted reactions towards the gesture. German writer Günther Grass recalled: "I remember the moment of panic and thought that something unexpected has just happened." Mieczysław Rakowski noted: "Indeed, it has become something great, historical. I felt tears coming into my eyes. Returning in the car from the monument with the members of the German delegation, I could not extort myself or a single word. Brandt surprises us, he deserves our respect and admiration." The wife of Prime Minister Cyrankiewicz was also moved to tears—like her husband—as if she was the prisoner of many wartime German camps.

As the visit of Willy Brandt and his delegation ended, the news reached West Germany—also about the gesture. The initial opinions here were mixed. Some praised for Brandt's courage and for the Ostpolitik policy. Others felt that Brandt's gesture was too exaggerated. The original name for it, the *Kniefall*, indicated not just kneeling, but *genuflection*, falling on the soil, an act of submission. Meanwhile, the domestic Polish media were initially silent about the gesture. Some critics bitterly remarked that Brandt kneeled "in front of the wrong monument"—referring that the chancellor knelt in front of a monument commemorating Jewish and not Polish victims of the War. The immediate positive feedback that the German Chancellor received came from the international audience. In Western Europe, the *Kniefall* was compared with a meeting between chancellor Adenauer and French president Charles de Gaulle in 1963, which marked German-French reconciliation. The *American Time* Magazine declared Brandt the Man of the Year, and the Stockholm Committee chose him for the Nobel Peace Prize in 1971.

And what did Willy Brandt think about all of this? After coming back to Germany and being asked by his wife, he brushed the question saying "someone had to do this, everything else would be too small (symbolically)". He added later: "I begged for forgiveness for my nation and prayed for the grace of redemption." In his memoirs, he noted: "I hadn't planned anything but had left Wilanow Palace, where I was staying, with the feeling that I had to do something to commemorate the special nature of the ceremony by the Ghetto Monument. (…) Under the abyss of German history and the weight of millions of murdered people I did what people do when words fail them."

The German Chancellor and the German delegation clearly understood the significance of the Ghetto Heroes Monument. We could say that he and the German delegation recognized that it was an important site of memory within a site of memory. As witnesses noted, the visit of the German Chancellor in Warsaw—a site of memory of Poland experience during World War II—had already symbolic implications. The power of the gesture went even further—it addressed one of the most tragic episodes in Warsaw and Poland history, the fate of Jewish Ghetto fighters and Polish Jews in general. The *Kniefall* was rather a spontaneous expression, however, a spontaneous expression at a well selected place.

Contrary to popular beliefs, the *Kniefall* was not accepted by everybody from the start. And precisely that feature made it even more groundbreaking. Simmilar to the case of Polish bishops, Willy Brandt's action transgressed concerns of contemporary politics. Even if the initial response was not always welcoming, as the time passed, both the letter and the *Kniefall* became the cornerstones for the reconciliation.

Compared to the letter, the *Kniefall* appeared in the context of the Warsaw Treaty of the 1970. If the *Kniefall* was an important gesture in symbolic and moral terms, then the Warsaw Treaty played a role as a legal document stabilizing the Polish-German relations. As Jerzy Wiatr observed, the border treaty helped relaxing public perception of the Germans in Poland. "In the nineteen-sixties and particularly in the nineteen-seventies (after the Warsaw Agreement of 1970), more differentiated views began to prevail. The negative perception of Germany began to fade, at least partly." Since the border was secured, the fear of potential conflict gradually diminished.

It was a breakthrough in Polish-German reconciliation indeed, a breakthrough in which Warsaw played its role. Initially, it helped in organizing informal contacts between different reconciliatory groups. At the time of the Letter of Polish Bishops to German Bishops, Warsaw was described as "left in ruins" and mentioned in the context of broader suffering of Polish nation. At the time of the *Kniefall*, the gesture made by Willy Brandt also addressed city's experience with the War.

The progress was made, however, It took time to comprehend the significance of what happened—and what could be done more.

Reflecting on the Past for Peace

Naturally, the Letter of Polish Bishops of 1965 and the *Kniefall* by Willy Brandt of 1970 did not mean the end of the reconciliation process. As we saw it, these milestones were met at a time with a lot of skepticism—both in Poland and in Germany. In addition, the political climate was still hampering further steps in reconciliation. The dominant rhetoric of the Eastern Bloc was still the "fighting for peace" narrative. Congresses of Wroclaw of 1948 and Warsaw of 1950 paved the way for the establishment of the World Peace Council. Financed by the USSR, the Council organized yearly conferences in a similar formula to those prepared in Wroclaw and Warsaw.

Despite the "fighting for peace" prevailing and initial limited response to the letter and the *Kniefall*, government diplomatic relations between Poland and West Germany continue to improve. With the ratification of the Warsaw Treaty in 1972, the two countries officially established diplomatic relations. The Polish government under Edward Gierek adopted a more relaxed approach towards Western countries. In 1975, Gierek and the new West-German Chancellor Helmut Schmidt prolonged a new agreement which established economic cooperation between the countries. The agreement also allowed former German citizens in Poland to visit the Federal Republic of Germany if they intented to reunite with the families.

New initiatives appeared in education too. In 1970, during the general conference of UNESCO in Paris, the two sides agreed on establishing a joint commission. The initiative was finalized after the Warsaw Treaty in 1972. Jerzy Wiatr described the role of the commission, "free the textbooks from contents harmful to the process of mutual understanding and to influence the process of education in a way conducive to mutual understanding between the two nations". The commission had two chairmans. The German side chose Georg Eckert, who was at the time the president of the German UNESCO Commission and the International Textbook Institute (Internationales Schulbuchinstitut). Meanwhile, the Polish side was represented by Władysław Markiewicz, a sociology professor and the director of the Western Institute. Established in Poznań, the Western Institute (Instytut Zachodni) was and is a research unit dedicated to the Polish-German relations.

The commission prolonged recommendations regarding history textbooks in 1977. Jerzy Wiatr stated that one recommendation included "the elimination of negative stereotypes and filling gaps in the knowledge of history". The commission faced different limitations: both countries at the time had different education systems. Despite that, it was one of many initiatives which bolstered mutual Polish-German common understanding. Furthermore—it touched upon one of primary sources of the conflict between the two nations—the complicated past and how it was narrated.

The rise of the Solidarity Movement and the fall of Edward Gierek in 1980 opened a new political era and changes in memorization. The new stage of discussion also happened in Germany. The SPD remained in power until the Christian Democratic Union under the new chancellor Helmut Kohl in 1982, which also brought a new vision towards national history.

The new chancellor—along with 1980s prominent historians such as Michael Sturmer—asked the following question—what is our identity as Germans? It was an important inquiry. Especially during the 1960s and the 1970s, which roughly corresponded with the SPD era, the Germans mostly focused on understanding their guilt using negating former ideas towards history. However, the attitude could not last forever, as the nation nevertheless needed to have an identity based on a common history. The question was important as the Eastern German neighbor—as it was noticed—also slowly reexamined history by returning to national symbols. The statue of Frederic the Great, once a symbol of Prussian reactionary, returned to Berlin after a long absence. Western intellectuals were prompted to reexamine the history of the country once again, also by looking at the difficult heritage of the Prussian State. On the Polish side, the "Prussian problem" discussed by Stanisław Stomma, one of the main intellectuals who contributed to the Polish-German reconciliation. In 1980, he wrote *Czy Fatalizm wrogości? Refleksje o stosunkach polsko-niemieckich 1871-1933* (The Fatalism of Hostility? Reflections upon Polish-German Relations 1871-1933).

Stomma's analysis is worth to be considered in detail. To some extend, *Czy fatalizm wrogości* used and reflected upon works of German historians such as Golo Mann, Ralf Dahrendorf, Fritz Fischer and many others. In this light, we may perceive Stomma's work in a broader debate over Germany's past at that time. What is more, the book was important for the debates at the time regarding the Polish-German relations. When the book was published in 1980, it was common in Polish public discourse to link Polish-German relations with the tragic experience of World War II. Some commentators went even further, claiming that the catastrophe of the War was rooted in older past. First antagonisms were traced even back to the medieval land of Prussia. However, was the Polish-German hostility inevitable? Furthermore, was such a hostility destined to prevail?

By starting his analysis, Stomma claimed that the disaster of World War II had different consequences for Poland and Germany. "An aggression, which struck Poland in 1939, unleashed a storm ending in a catastrophe of dimensions rarely seen in history." As a result of the disastrous war, the interwar Polish state (and, what also concerns us in this book, Warsaw) were utterly destroyed. Meanwhile, for Germany, World War II was in fact a second catastrophe: the first came during World War I. They both constituted a final blow to a certain model of the German state which primarily took shape in a period between 1871 and 1933. When reflecting on Germany's past, Stomma put forward a question: "Can it be concluded that these major catastrophic events were accidental, that different, unique sets of special circumstances were at work each time? And if not, what were the mechanisms of the events? What were the recurring sets of facts?"

As we noticed, when we talked about Germany's past, one term appeared very often: Prussia. Originally, the term denoted a landmass between the Vistula and Neman Rivers. It was home to indigenous tribes who were collectively known as Prussians or the Old-Prussians. For dukes of Masovia and other rulers within medieval Poland, the Prussians were a difficult neighbor. Prussian war bands often entered Polish lands for raid and pillage. In addition, religious differences also played the role in generating tension as the Prussians were one of the last tribes in medieval Europe who adhered to pre-Christian belief system.

One Polish duke—Konrad I of Masovia—decided to find a solution to the problem. In 1226, duke Konrad invited representatives of a knight order which was formed in Palestine, at the time of the Crusades. This order, commonly known as the Teutonic Knights (or the *Deutscher Orden* - The German Order), was offered by the duke of Masovia a piece of land. In exchange, the knights were assigned with a mission to prevent further attacks coming from the Prussian tribes. In an unexpected turn for the Polish side, the Teutonic Order soon expanded, to the point it dominated the Baltic Region from the 13th to the 15th century. However, the Order eventually succumbed to the Kingdom of Poland after a series of wars. In the war of 1409-1411, Polish-Lithuanian forces defeated the Teutonic Knights at the battle of Grunwald. During the later war of 1454-1466, the Order was significantly weakened.

In 1517, the last Grand Master of the Teutonic Order established himself as a prince of the Hohenzollern dynasty and a vassal of the Polish king. The Teutonic state disappeared and was replaced by a Prussian Duchy. Throughout the 16th and 17th centuries, the Prussian Duchy remained a vassal of the Polish Kingdom and later of the Polish-Lithuanian Commonwealth. As a result of Polish-Swedish war of 1655-1660, the Duchy of Prussia ceased to be the Polish vassal in 1657. In 1701, the Duchy of Prussia merged with the Brandenburg Electorate to became one entity—the Kingdom of Prussia.

Stomma, along with the German historians observed that the Prussian Kingdom shaped the future character of Imperial Germany (1871-1918), the Weimar Republic (1918-1933) and the Nazi Germany (1933-1945). Without going too deep into history, we may see what features of Prussian state that Stomma pointed out in his analysis.

From the very beginning, the Prussian Kingdom developed its military. The army preserved Prussia's sovereignty from larger competitors such as Austria. However, the role of the military exceeded the one related to national security: it was also a force enabling quick territorial expansion. Prussia grew in its territory, annexing the land of Silesia from Austria and taking part in partitions of Polish-Lithuanian Commonwealth. An emphasis of the army development eventually gave birth to the Prussian style militarism. As Stomma and German historian Emil Oberman observed, the Prussian military functioned as a distinct entity. Prussian officers were an autonomous, if not a separate caste within the Prussian society. Officers together with soldiers had a great impact on the national policy. Here, however, the situation in Prussia went one step further.

Militaristic tendencies eventually gave a rise of a particular posture of the ruling military class in Prussia. Stanisław Stomma and others called it *Preussentum*, which Annike Frieberg translated as "the Prussianism". "It is difficult to talk about the Prussian nation. *Preussentum* is a way of behavior, political type, and political-administrative system." Stomma believed that the observers could not point out to the particular region within the Prussian state which could identify itself as "Prussian". Instead, it were the officers who identified themselves as Prussian. They usually were the Junckers, a special type of nobility that combined the lifestyle of landowners with cultivating military strength. There was no region that was Prussia's heartland, it was country's officers which exercised the *Preussentum*. Which is why Stomma concluded in his analysis that: "Prussia was rather a political than a geographical term, rather a system than a country." The *Preussentum* emphasized an army-like discipline in governing the country, for which there was little space for critical thinking. Soldiers had to obey uncritically their offcers, in turn, the officers had to obey the central command. In this vision, Prussian society also existed for the sake of the support of its army. To illustrate this point, Stomma quoted a popular saying from the era: "Prussia is not a country with an army, rather, it is an army with a country."

This "army with a country" proved resilient to changes and challenges. The Napoleonic Wars wreaked havoc on lands controlled by the Prussian Kingdom. Despite this, the Juncker caste which embodied *Preussentum* survived: Prussian officers helped reconstructing the country after the Vienna Congress of 1815. In 1848, a series of events called the Spring of the Nations challenged traditional monarchies in Europe. In Prussia, the liberal-minded politicians organized a parliament and proposed a constitutional monarchy of the unified Germany. However, the Prussian King Frederic Wilhelm IV refused and the army supressed the liberal revolution. We could say that if the liberals wanted state power and the military to obey to the people, a very different situation occurred: the liberals eventually had to submit to the army and the king. As Stomma suggested, similar developments happened later: there was no successful revolution which could destroy the *Preussentum*. The system proved adaptive too: even though the officers were less and less influential economically, they were still backed by the emerging class of capitalists. Big business owners supported financially the Prussian state, in exchange, the military offered protection to Prussian companies.

Ultimately, it was the Prussian military machine, and not idealistic German liberal that unified German states into one country. In 1866, the Prussian army achieved a decisive victory over Austria during the battle of Königgrätz (also known as Sadowa). Victorious Prussia formed the North German Confederation. In 1870, the Confederation and southern German states jointly declared war on France. After one year, the North-German forces were victorious; humiliated France lost the Alsace-Lorraine region. In January 1871, Prussian King Wilhelm proclaimed himself the first Emperor of Germany. An new empire was formed and the Prussianism became its system. It was a new development: throughout centuries, Germany appeared more as a mosaic of numerous states rather than being a coherent political organism. The Holy Roman Empire that existed from the Middle Ages until the Napoleonic Wars was a good example of it. The Holy Roman Emperor was rather first among the equal, one who could influence, but could not control other monarchs of German states. By contrast, the Imperial

Germany was a much more unified entity where the Prussianism played the key role. But, as Stomma observed, a particular phenomenon completed the *Preussentum*. He and historian Hans Heigert called this strain of thought the philosophical idealism or, if less complex— irrationalism.

For Stomma and Heigert, the idealism or irrationalism manifested itself in the 19th century romanticism. The romantic literature emphasized the feeling over the reason. Its writers were fascinated with the mystery found in myths, history and folk culture. However, the idealism/irrationalism element was more than a part of romanticism. Stomma and Heigert argued that fascination over the mythical past created a contempt over the present. Such a contempt of the present caused German romantics to support institutions associated with the past—the German army, the church, the monarch. An irrational thought was also present in domains not related to original literature context. Stanisław Stomma described after German historian Helga Grebbing and Erich Muller-Gangloff another term, the "overcompensation" or *Überkompensation*. Stomma described it as "one of radical forms of German nationalism" which appeared after formation of the Imperial Germany in 1871 and which later influenced Nazi ideology. Before the 19th century, Germany was not a unified political organism, rather a constellation of different German states. Such a situation created a "loophole in history", and, in turn, a need to "psychologically compensate the lacking of the past".

Such a tradition of an irrational way of thinking influenced future decisions. After 1871, Otto von Bismarck became a chancellor of the Imperial Germany. Despite being a juncker and a conservative, Bismarck policies were pragmatic. He understood that Germany should maintain balance between the powers and avoid an open confrontation. The situation changed when the new emperor Wilhelm II ascended the throne in 1888. During his reign, Germany adopted the *Weltpolitik* (world politics). The German leaders planned turning their country into the great power. They pursued the goal by engaging in colonial wars, competing with other countries and pursuing other imperialist policies. This antagonistic approach led to a conflict between Wilhelm II and Otto von Bismarck which resulted in German Chancellor stepping down from his position in 1890. German foreign affairs were to be decided by the emperor and the military.

When it came to foreign affairs at that time Germany, along with the United Kingdom, France and Russia were the main players in European politics. The question remained on how Germany wanted to form its alliances. Among mentioned great powers, France could not befriend Germany. Since the humiliation in Franco-Prussian War of 1870-1871, the leaders of the French state saw its eastern neighbor as a mortal enemy. Any alliance would be impossible. Therefore, as Stomma and German historians accessed, the German strategy should consider befriending one of remaining major powers. Measures attempting to ally with Russia failed: an increasing military strength of the German Empire made Russia more keen aligning with other countries. In addition, Germany reapproached Austria-Hungary after unification war—the two formed a military alliance. Here, the German leaders had to consider Austria-Hungarian ambitions. The dual monarchy was traditionally interested in expansion over the Balkans. As Russia also had its interest in the region, this led inevitably to Russian-Austrian conflict. Consequently, since Germany sided with the Austrians, Russo-German relations further deteriorated. Facing the potential German peril, the Russian Empire eventually befriended France.

Alternatively, the United Kingdom seemed to be a potential candidate for an ally of the Imperial Germany. Despite that, kaiser Wilhelm favored the move which antagonized the UK against Germany—naval expansion. Traditionally, the UK was used to its naval superiority, the "Britannia rules the waves" slogan being an encapsulation of this mentality. Before his dismissal, Chancellor Bismarck warned the young emperor not to expand the German High Fleet (*Hochseeflottee*) as the move could enrage the British. However, Kaiser Wilhelm was not willing to listen. He and the admirals made the erroneous assumption that the German-British conflict was to be inevitable. Building a strong fleet—in their opinion—should have forced England to cooperate. The decision also followed tendencies of *überkompensation* and broader irrational/idealistic thought. The German High Seas Fleet under admiral Alfred von Tirpitz was to bring a sense of pride to Imperial Germany. Contrary to expectations, the UK decided to ally France precisely because of the military pressure coming from the German Empire.

Thus Germany became surrounded by the triple alliance of great powers which later would be known as the Entente. What finally cemented the fate of the German Empire was increasing pro-war propaganda within the country. For some military strategists, war with other great powers was inevitable, moreover, it should be considered as a method of prevention. In their opinion, a war could be a prevention from Russia becoming too strong in the future. They also believed that a war with France could be a prevention from coordinated French-Russian attack on German soil. The war plan proposed by the Chief of Staff general Alfred von Schlieffen (commonly known by the contemporaries as the Schlieffen Plan) had this notion of preemptive strike. According to the plan, the German Army should defeat the French forces first before it would be possible to combat Russia.

Stanisław Stomma together with German historians called above described decisions as the reversal of the classical concept of the war. Clausewitz and other classical theorists viewed war and the military force as an extension of politics. However, in case of the Imperial Germany, politics became an extension of army calculations, the Schlieffen Plan and the German Navy expansion both being the best examples of it. The tendency was driven by an inability of Wilhelm II and the German high command to look into the motivations of Russia and England. That inability eventually doomed the Empire.

On 28th June 1914, the Austria-Hungarian archduke Franz Ferdinand was assassinated by a Serbian nationalist Gavrilo Princip. On the same day, Austria-Hungary declared a war on Serbia. For Stomma and the historians he cited, Austria-Hungarian monarchy's gesture was an act of desperation to preserve the crumbling country's integrity. The German high command supported the move of Austria and decided to implement preventive measures against adversaries, erroneously interpreting the war as inevitable. When Russia declared mobilization as a tool to increase pressure over Austria-Hungary, German politicians still had options to prevent the conflict. However, the fatalistic approach convinced them to declare war on Russia.

World War I was the first catastrophe for Germany. After 1918, the Kaiser abdicated, the country was forced to sign a Treaty of Versailles and had to accept the resurrection of Poland as its neighbor. However, how paradoxical it may look, the core political model for the Weimar Republic was not too different from the German Empire. The Kaiser did abdicate and the parliament was to have a better role. However, Prussia and the Prussianism were still to be the force rallying the country. The Revolution of 1918-1919 was put down by social democrats and the remaining German military. The newly formed Weimar Republic still had to rely on Prussian ideas of governing the country, since the army guaranteed its existence. After 1925-1926, the Prussian element once again rose in power. Wartime hero field marshal Paul von Hinderburg replaced deceased Friedrich Ebert as Germany's president in 1925. The financial crisis drew public opinion towards the sympathy of conservative and Nazi politicians.

The end of World War I was the end of Imperial Germany, but the beginning for the Polish Second Republic. In 1918, the Poles launched a successful Greater Poland Uprising, which convinced the foreign powers to cede territory to the new Polish Republic. The Poles also launched three Silesian Uprisings (1919-1921) that resulted in partition of Silesia between Poland and Germany. Lastly, Poland received access to the sea, effectively splitting Eastern Prussia region from the rest of Germany. When the border was finally regulated in 1922, a significant percentage of lands formerly controlled by the Imperial Germany was now in hands of Poland. Some could think that the Weimar Republic and the Polish Second Republic should maintain friendly relations since the two countries were democracies. This was far from being true: the two sides had a hostile attitude towards one another. The antagonism revolved around the border issue. For the new German Republic, Poland divided the territory of Germany into two parts—the German mainland and remaining Prussia around the city of Konigsberg. Moreover, Poland took away territories which were valuable economically for the Imperial Germany. The Greater Poland was a large agricultural base whereas the Upper Silesia became an important industrial region. For Poland, no matter if it was the Greater Poland, Silesia, or the Baltic Sea, all these lands were to be considered historically Polish.

The rising nationalism in both countries did not help in this situation either. In Germany, nationalist tendencies were to worsen due to the rise of fascism. In 1919, a small German Workers Party (Deutscher Arbeiterpartei, the DAP) was formed. Its member Adolf Hitler eventually became the new leader. The DAP was renamed to National Socialist German Workers Party (Nationalsocialistische Deutsche Arbeitpareit, the NSDAP). The NSDAP became more recognizable under its contracted name: the Nazi party. For Stanisław Stomma, the Nazis utilized fully the potential of the *Preussentum*. Originally, many Prussianist politicians despised the Nazis. For aristocratic Juncker military commanders such as Hindenburg, the Nazis were low-class Bavarians unworthy to govern the country. Despite that, when Hitler won the elections of 1933, Hinderburg appointed him as a new chancellor. One year later Hinderburg passed away, and Hitler was elevated to the position of Fuhrer. The Nazis would praise the Prussian militarism and make political rallies dedicated to it. At the same time, generals who were Prussians (that is, adherents to *the Preussentum*) followed Hitler's orders. Stomma commented that "the hitlerism was not a child of the Juncker caste". The Nazi ideology appeared independently from the Prussianist tradition. However, "many people of the Juncker class did form an alliance with hitlerism and went on service for it". It was only during the later stage of World War II that some of Junckers "decided to cancel this alliance and started rebelling against Hitler".

For Stomma and the German historians, the Nazis utilized the character of the former Prussian state. Moreover, Hitler and the NSDAP also exploited tendencies which existed within the German society. They further embraced previously described nationalism and idealism, taking it one step further. As Stomma noted, an irrational idolizing certain ideas which could be described as a fetishism of words "existed way before the national socialism". The concepts of fidelity, discipline, a nation (*der Volk*) were commonly used and venerated in Imperial Germany. The veneration usually came without any criticism, without any explanation of what these words actualy mean. "The kind of danger, which the tendency to idolize concepts concealed, came to the light during the rise of fascism in Germany."

This rise of fascism eventually gave increased hostility between Poland and Germany that, in turn, erupted during World War II. For Stomma, hostility between the Poles and the Germans did exist. Its roots could be found in earlier history, in this case, in history of Prussia and the Imperial Germany. However, was this hostility destined to happen? Here, Stomma disagreed. He argued that in the course of German history, we could imagine alternative scenarios happening. Germany could have been united by an political entity other than Prussia: the Austrian Empire being an example of it. Stomma also considered the question if World War I could have been prevented. Based on German historians' analysis, he claimed that there was no "inevitable determinism of facts which dragged Austria-Hungary into war. It is not true either that there was any fatal chain of objective causes that forced Germany into implementing the Schlieffen plan". Stomma analyzed reasons for Prussian and German politicians' acting one way over another. These reasons included: nationalism, the *Preussentum*, irrationalism and the *Überkompensation*, the erroneous decisions made prior to the war. However, Stomma rejected the idea of fatalism, that World War I was for Germany inevitable. "Peace and war are matters of political choice. Wrong and perniciously misleading are notions which equate peace with passive political action. It is precisely a belief in automatism of facts which can lead to war. Peace is always somehow politically conditioned. For every historical context, the choice between peace and war always looks different."

Therefore, even though the appearance of the Nazi Germany was grounded in history, multiple possible scenarios showed that the "Nazi scenario" was not the only option. Similarly, Stanisław Stomma argued that the Polish-German hostility was not necessarily destined to happen. There were several cases where the two sides could have had friendlier relations. What were they? For these, he concentrated his analysis on 3 possible scenarios: a potential alliance between Prussia and the Polish-

Lithuanian Commonwealth in 1790, the 5th November Act of 1916 made by Imperial Germany regarding Polish independence, friendly relations between the Weimar Republic and the Polish Second Republic. Despite these alternative scenarios failed, they nevertheless indicated a possibility of a less antagonistic and more peaceful Polish-German relations.

For one scenario Stanisław Stomma made an exemption. He dismissed the idea of friendlier relations between the Nazi Germany and the Polish Second Republic. During first years of its existence, the Nazi Germany seemed to have implemented more relaxed foreign policy towards its Polish neighbor. The German Prime Minister Joachim von Ribbentrop and the German Field Marshall Herman Göring were frequent guests in Warsaw. They were persuading Poland to join the Anti-Comintern Pact. However, Poland simply could not accept any political alliance which required ceding its national territory to the German neighbor. Polish Minister of Foreign Affairs Ludwik Beck could not agree to return Gdańsk/Danzig back to Germany. He could not agree to a proposal of forming an exterritorial land, so that the main part of Germany could have a link with remaining Prussia. The Anti-Comintern Pact was not a feasible perspective either. Poland maintained a policy of equal distance towards the Nazi Germany and the Soviet Union, unwilling to side with any of the two neighbors. For Hitler and his subordinates, friendly gestures were just an attempt to save time for a future invasion.

In a way, Adolf Hitler and the Nazi Party rouse upon earlier territorial disputes. "After the defeat of 1918, a nightmare of German politicians became the reality: an independent Polish state appeared with Greater Poland region and Pomerania on its side. The territorial integrity of the Prussian (also German) state was broken." It is no wonder then the territorial dispute led to hostility. However, "was the situation couldn't be reversed? Was it an inevitable historical fatalism that was in charge?" To this, Stomma disagreed. For him, the determinism suggests that objective circumstances logically suggest a certain option. That was not the case for the rise of the Nazi Germany and the Polish-German hostility. Even if objective geopolitical elements played the role, the hostility was also a result of decisions of individuals. "So, there is no fatalism of geopolitics. From the very same situation one can draw different conclusions." By analogy, Stanisław Stomma provided another example outside of the Polish-German context: the rise of the Imperial Japan. The Japanese Imperialists justified their expansion during World War II by presenting objective geopolitical circumstances. They attempted justifying the aggression against China, Southeast Asian countries and the United States by pointing to lack of resource, the need to find new markets, to "secure" the Japanese nation. But, for Stomma, the post-war history of Japan suggested that a peaceful, non-antagonistic existence of Japan with its neighbors could be possible. Making a different choice also means challenging one's way of thinking, but it is possible.

Thus, for Stanisław Stomma, an analysis of history could also be helpful in imagining peaceful alternatives, a way to overcome the hostility. However, he indicated limitations of such analysis. "All, that we know, cannot explain atrocities. We are approaching sort of psychological barrier that was crossed. We cannot explain the full enormity of atrocities, neither in social nor psychological categories." Stomma himself reflected on his own experiences regarding the Nazi war crimes in

Vilnius region, where the local Jewish population was exterminated. To him, examining the past could explain sources of the hostility, but not the scale of terror goes beyond such explanations. The atrocities themselves were not grounded in any particular "predispositions" of the German nation or culture. "We see no such predispositions. What is left is a phenomenon—the black spot in history, the fact of evil in terrifying sizes." The rise of the Nazi ideology and subsequent tragedies of World War II were to Stomma a historical fact. It was also clear to him that "the German nation did not prove itself immune when facing an invasion of the evil. It let the evil found the nest and spread around its own national body. A serious warning to all of the peoples around the world." Such an evil may occur in any nation or among other peoples. Which is why, for Stomma, we should be cautious of the evil "roaring like a lion, seeking for someone to devour".

The end of World War II marked the new beginning for Polish-German relations. *Czy Fatalizm Wrogości?* briefly outlined the progress of the reconciliation and different groups partaking in it. By concluding his work, Stomma called for more undertakings on Polish-German reconciliation. As he stated: "This case is worth the effort."

Despite not mentioning Warsaw, Stanisław Stomma's *Czy Fatalizm Wrogości?* reflected indirectly on what happened in Poland and it's capital during World War II. Stomma wrote his book in 1980, 10 years after Brandt's *Kniefall*. This is why he probably added the question mark to his book: at that time, some people may have still wondered if the Polish-German relations were destined to be hostile. As Stomma presented, although the past hostility existed, it was not a fatal one after all. This, in turn, gives a hope that the hostility can be overcome and that the reconciliation is, after all possible. Understanding the past can be a tool for this overcoming.

Reconsidering was not limited to the intellectuals such as Stanisław Stomma. It was also a concern for other actors involved, one of the hierarchs of the Catholic Church. In 1978, Polish cardinal Karol Wojtyła was elected as the new pope. Upon the conclave which elected him, he took the name of John Paul II. In 1979, the pope made an official visit to Poland. During his speech at the Victory Square in 1979 in Warsaw, he commented on the city's wartime experience:

> *It is impossible without Christ to understand this nation with its past so full of splendour and also of terrible difficulties. It is impossible to understand this city, Warsaw, the capital of Poland, that undertook in 1944 an unequal battle against the aggressor, a battle in which it was abandoned by the allied powers, a battle in which it was buried under its own ruins—if it is not remembered that under those same ruins there was also the statue of Christ the Saviour with his cross that is in front of the church at Krakowskie Przedmiescie. There is no way to understand this nation, which has had a past so great, but at the same time so horribly difficult—without Christ. There is no way to understand this city, Warsaw, the capital of Poland, which in the year 1944 decided on an uneven fight against the invaders, the struggle in which it was abandoned by Allied Powers, the struggle, in which it fell under its own ruins, if he does not remember that under the same ruins Christ the Savior fell with his cross before the church in Krakowskie Przedmieście.*

As the leader of the Catholic Church, the pope John Paul II praised the bravery of Warsaw and its Warsaw people: their actions made them become martyrs. The pope referred to the statue of Jesus Christ of the Holy Cross Church in Warsaw which was damaged during World War II. Despite damages, it survived the war and was renovated afterwards. The pope ended with a call for a renewal and changes in the country: "Let your Spirit descend. Let your Spirit descend and renew the face of the earth, the face of this land."

Even though the speech did not directly reflect upon peace and reconciliation, it did reflect upon the past of Warsaw and Poland. Moreover, the Pope John Paul II influenced ideas of peace and reconciliation in Poland during the time of changes.

Peace and Reconciliation at the Time of Transformation

The late 1970s and early 1980s marked the beginning of changes. Poland still faced the impact of economic crisis after Edward Gierek's rule. The country endured a political crisis too: after the abolition of the martial law of 1983, tensions between the governmental side led by general Wojciech Jaruzelski on one side, and the opposition mostly led by the outlawed Solidarity Movement continued to exist.

In these turbulent times, the United Nations declared in November 1981 the celebration of the International Peace Day starting from 1982. In addition, the UN General Assembly declared 1986 to become the International Year of Peace. As the Resolution No. 37/16 stated, the International Year of Peace was declared based upon a consideration "that the promotion of peace is the basic objective of the United Nations" and on recognition "that peace continues to be a goal instead of an achievement, despite the resolute efforts of the United Nations". Moreover, it invited "all States, all organizations within the United Nations system and interested non-governmental organizations to exert all possible efforts for the preparation and observance of the International Year of Peace". In other words, the UN encouraged all parties to host peace activities celebrating the peace year of 1986.

Poland was one of the signatory countries of the United Nations Charter and has been a member of the organization from the beginning. Moreover, it hosted peace related activities, Wrocław Congress of 1948 and Warsaw Congress of 1950 being notable examples. However, the events were not related to the peace movement organized around the UN. Instead, conferences held in Wrocław and Warsaw were precursors of later similar activities which were organized by the Soviet-led World Peace Council. These congresses largely followed the "fighting for peace" narrative, so peculiar to the Eastern Bloc countries. This time, however, the governmental side in Poland planned a conference which was not affiliated with the World Peace Council.

Finally, the initiative was proposed under the name "Congress of Intellectuals for a Peaceful Future of the World". In official material for the Congress, the organizers presented reasons behind hosting the event: "The deterioration of the international situation in the late 1970s and early 1980s brought a new life to peace activity. The awareness of the growing threat of a nuclear conflict was accompanied by the realization of dangers posed by the devastation of man's natural environment, the rapacious exploitation of natural resources, and the unjust system of international economic relations." Because of that, a group of "Polish writers and scholars decided to convene an international meeting of intellectuals devoted to broadly conceived problems of peace". The conference committee was established in 1983 and chose Bogdan Suchodolski as its chairman.

Bogdan Suchodolski was a pedagogue, philosopher, and a well established professor working for the Polish Academy of Sciences. He thought that the role of the Congress and its intellectuals should be finding ways of promoting peace via education foremost. An interview with him was featured in the Congress's official brochure. Here, Suchodolski presented his opinion: "The point is that we realize that the future should not be a continuation of contemporaneity. Such a future would lead to a catastrophe. We should strive for a new future, a different future." He emphasized the need for the intellectuals to cooperate together. By forming a backbone of the peace education, they could educate people regarding potential threat to peace: arms race, nuclear war, climate change, discrimination being among them. "They should try to convince the people that something must be done to save our common world. Only intellectuals can do this."

For such a congress, Poland was a preferable location. As Suchodolski argued: "Poland, the country probably most painfully affected by fascism and the war, has a moral right to tell the world: Look, what the war was like, what the fascism was like." Suchodolski himself believed in "idea of tolerance, faith in shaping relations between nations, not according to the Teutonic Knights model, but on principles of justice, respect for the rights of other people". References to "fascism" and "Teutonic Knights" were common for the "fighting for peace" narrative in the Polish People's Republic. Emphasizing Warsaw as a victim of fascism could be seen back during the World Congress of the Supporters of Peace of 1950. Despite these two terms being commonly used in "fighting for peace" rhetoric, Bogdan Suchodolski further explained his position in separate paper entitled *Wychowanie Dla Pokoju* (Peace Education, Peace Upbringing). He criticized ideologies such as fascism as "anti-humanist ideologies" which "classified people and nations of this Earth into superior and inferior ones, those to be privileged and those to be discriminated". Teutonic knights also fell into this category: Suchodolski mentioned in his writings, Paweł Włodkowic—the very same theologian who debated Teutonic knights representatives.

Without going further into details, we might read Suchodolski's ideas for the Congress as a call for peace education which the intellectuals are morally obliged to do. Here, Poland played the role as a nation which experienced violence of anti-humanist ideologies. For Scuhodolski, such a moral obligation required intellectuals (especially Polish ones) to educate younger generations. If successful, the peace education could prevent younger generations from repeating the past. "If we organize this Congress, it is, above all, out of obedience to the dictates of our conscience, which requires people who perhaps descry reality more keenly than others to bear witness to the truth. We must say what this world is like, what threatens us, and how to save the world."

The Committee under Bogdan Suchodolski promoted the Congress with the authorities of the Polish People's Republic. In 1984, the committee issued an appeal "to scientists and artists". The appeal reiterated challenges that Congress was to discuss: the threat of war, climate change, socio-economic imbalances around the world being among them. The appeal recalled the 1948 World Congress of Intellectuals in Defense of Peace held in Wrocław as one of inspirations for hosting the event in Warsaw. The organizer linked heavily the initiative with the United Nations, also with the International Year of Peace that the UN announced. During the 40th session of the General Assembly of the UN in April 1985, The First Secretary of the PUWP Wojciech Jaruzelski endorsed the initiative on behalf of the Polish government at the time.

The Warsaw Congress [Fig.3-5], officially known as "the Congress of Intellectuals for a Peaceful Future of the World" was hosted from January 16th to 19th 1986. The organizer stressed the official support from the General Secretary of the UN Javier Perez de Cuellar, official Polish authorities, foreign officials, politicians and intellectuals. The participants mostly included representatives of the Eastern Bloc Countries. Other guests included the Swedish Premier Olof Palme, the former UN Secretary Kurt Waldheim, Archbishop Achille Silvestrini on behalf of Pope John Paul II, the Director-General of the UNESCO Amadou-Mahtar M'Bow. Some representatives sent their messages for the occasion, among them were Mayor of Nagasaki Masahiko Ikeda and Wang Bingnan, who at the time was Chairman of the Committee of the International Year of Peace in the People's Republic of China. The Polish People's Republic government was represented by Marshall of the Sejm Roman Malinowski and Vice-Marshall of the Sejm Mieczysław Rakowski.

Fig.3-5 The Congress of Intellectuals for a Peaceful Future of the World. Bogdan Suchodolski (center) speaking during the session.

The Congress was split into working groups which debated several topics. These included: the international peace and security, the protection of the environment and health, the global prospects of economy, the preservation of common heritage of the humankind, the education for peace and actions in defense of peace. As the Marshall of the Sejm Roman Malinowski commented: "I am convinced that the intellectuals assembled here will arrive at conclusions which will constitute valuable premises in shaping man's thinking in such a way as to allow for hopeful and optimistic expectation of what the future might bring." In this context, Malinowski quoted John Paul II's New Year's address: "The problem of peace as a universal value (…) should be regarded with utmost intellectual honesty, sincerity of spirit, and a profound sense of responsibility before oneself and before the nations of the world."

The organizers also utilized Warsaw as a site of memory and linked it with the peace narrative. As the official summary of the Congress stated: "On January 17th, Warsaw celebrated the 41st anniversary of its liberation from the Nazi occupation. On that day, a group of participants in the Congress laid flowers at the monument of the Warsaw Nike, a symbol of the victory over fascism and war, a symbol of the reborn capital city." As Ewa Sztompke noted, the Warsaw Heroes Monument was at the time a popular place utilized by the authorities of Polish People's Republic during official anniversaries. Thus making the laying flowers ceremony in front of the "Nike" monument part of the Congress program was a logical consequence of an earlier practice [Fig.3-6].

Fig.3-6 The Congress of Intellectuals for a Peaceful Future of the World, 17th January 1986. A group of participants laid flowers in front of the Warsaw Heroes Monument.

However, utilizing Warsaw history did not end here. Such an undertaking also manifested in speeches conducted by the participants of the Congress. Roman Malinowski, who was at the time the Marshal of the Sejm (speaker of the lower house of the Polish parliament) remarked that, "the site of the Congress is no accident. Warsaw, the capital of Poland, was the first victim of the Nazi drive which resulted in World War II". As Malinowski argued, Warsaw stood out among other European cities as the one which "was destroyed methodically, in a planned manner, blasted and gutted, house after house, street after street, district after district during and following the crushing of the Warsaw Uprising". Here, the experience of Warsaw as well as the entire Poland was exceptional: Over six million Polish citizens—or every fifth person in our country—died and more than 40 percent of national assets were destroyed during the War.

The subject of Warsaw tragedy that Malinowski described was a prevailing topic of the conference. The General Secretary of the United Nations Javier Perez de Cuellar also commented on the subject. In his address, which was read by the vice secretary Yasushi Akashi, he emphasized that Warsaw "directly experienced the blow of wartime extermination". Compared to Malinowski, Perez de Cuellar stressed that since the end of World War II, Warsaw "has enjoyed peace, the value of which is particularly visible in the perspective of the past horrors of the conflict, which will never be forgotten". And for the General Secretary, it was precisely the post-war development of Warsaw that could be inspiring: "Among the destructive resorting to weapons that are still troubled by many parts of the world, the revived beauty of Warsaw reminds us what they can do in peace, people are energetic and capable of sacrifice."

Compared to Wroclaw Congress of 1948 and Warsaw Congress of 1950, the Congress of Intellectuals for a Peaceful Future of the World of 1986 was more grounded in the general peace agenda advocated by the United Nations. However, it was also an element of the broader "fighting for peace" narrative. Thus, the 1986 Congress shared similar problems of its predecessors, among them the politicized nature of the event. The critics who gathered around the Solidarity movement commented on the event. They believed that the Warsaw Congress of 1986 was an attempt to break international isolation. During an interview with Radio Free Europe, some of critics bitterly noted that choosing Warsaw as the place for hosting a congress of peace was inappropriate due to political repercussions after the Martial Law: "If this is how one understands the word *peace*, you will have to realize that you have come to a country in which there is no peace. You have come to a country in which war has been declared on their people by those who govern and who, without a trace of embarrassment, (sic.) bombard you with slogans of peace." The critics of the Congress also pointed out to the absence of many figures who were important to contemporary peace movement. Among some, there were the opposition leader the recipient of the Nobel Peace Prize Lech Wałęsa, the prime minister of Austria Bruno Kreisky, the German Chancellor Helmut Schmidt, the peace activist Pierre Joliot and many intellectuals from Norway and Sweden.

The Congress of Intellectuals for a Peaceful Future of the World, by large, was one of the last initiatives of its kind. With it, the long-lasting "fighting for peace" narrative, finally came to an end. The 1986 Warsaw Congress also marked a transition in what we may call an official peace culture. After the Congress, the promotion of peace culture became increasingly associated with international organizations such as the United Nations.

The International Year of Peace was an inspiration for the Congress of Intellectuals for a Peaceful Future of the World. However, it was not the only one. For their contributions to the World Peace, the United Nations conferred to cities around the world with the title of "Messengers of Peace". In 1988, in the final days of the Cold War, representatives of such cities held their general assembly in Verdun. Choosing Verdun as a place for the conference was a meaningful thing to do. This region witnessed in 1916 one of the most tragic episodes of World War I, a major clash between the French and German armies at the time. Decades later, in 1984, the French President Francois Mitterand and the German Chancellor Helmut Kohl visited Douaumont Ossuary Memorial near Verdun. During the memorial ceremony, two leaders of countries hold their hands together in a gesture of reconciliation. Few years later in 1988, the representatives of cities around the world, invited by Mayor of Verdun Jacques Barat-Dupont and under presence of the UN General Secretary Javier Perez de Cuellar formed the International Association of Peace Messenger Cities (IAPMC).

In the year 1989, the IAPMC hosted it's second general assembly—this time in Warsaw. Two days of the conference (1st and 2nd September) coincided with the 50th anniversary of World War II. During the event, the participants adopted the Warsaw Peace Appeal that was "read out at the Nike Monument". It stated that Warsaw "today is open to great hopes and which was the first victim of the Nazi German aggression". The appeal honored the "heroic city and its 800,000 killed inhabitants" and called for making considerations for a peaceful future. These considerations included: gradual reduction of armed forces, avoidance of conflicts threatening the world and creation of a collective security system which could be based on the UN Charter.

> *We, in this place, where armed resistance against the attackers was born, declare ourselves for containment and solving conflicts exclusively through dialogue and constructive negotiations.*

Apart from concerns regarding the security, the Warsaw Peace Appeal advocated for the world of greater pluralism which could be freed from the two opposed bloc mentality.

> *Our globe must become a real common home for all people independently of their colour, political and philosophical convictions or religion.*

The IAPMC also called for disavowing from confrontation to "search for the identity of Europe in pluralism and democracy, in rotations between states and peoples. May the right to life in peace come into force".

At the time when the IAPMC had it's general assembly in Warsaw, the Polish capital also joined another initiative. The Peace Bell, originally a gift of Japanese people to the United Nations in 1952, later became a widespread initiative. Warsaw received its own Peace Bell in 1989. Despite the original being stolen in 2002, a replica of the bell was presented to the public in 2015. [Fig.3-7]

The three above mentioned initiatives were inspired by the peace agenda of the United Nations. All three were distinctive in their respective ways. The 1986 Warsaw Congress was mostly an initiative organized by the Polish central government and by intellectuals endorsed by that government. By comparison, the General Assembly of the IAPMC and the the Peace Bell initiative mostly rallied regional governments, representatives of municipalities. Peace as a universal concept was promoted in Warsaw by various groups. Such initiatives, despite having little in common with the Polish-German reconciliation, nevertheless opened up possibilities for modelling a broader peace culture in Warsaw. Three initiatives occurred at the time of the transition period. The transition meant a next chapter in Polish history.

Fig.3-7 World Peace Bell in Warsaw. The original bell was cast and presented in 1989. Its copy stands today in Mokotów District.

During the time of the changes that occurred in the 1980s and 1990s, German Chancellor Helmut Kohl planned to visit Poland during the time of transformation.

As we mentioned before, the rise of Helmut Kohl and the CDU to power in the 1980s corresponded with changes within the German society. The new generation of Germans rethought the country's past. The discourse of German historians, which was summarized by Stanisław Stomma, examined origins of Nazi ideology as well as national hostilities. On political level, the new Chancellor of Germany also addressed the problem of the past. As Krystyna Kaczorowska in collective work *Msza pojednania w Krzyżowej* stated, Helmut Kohl tried balancing his stance. During his speech for the 40th anniversary of the Outbreak of World War II, "Helmut Kohl, on one hand, emphasized suffering of the

German 'expellees', on the other—he mentioned the necessity of the Polish-German reconciliation. He presented what was achieved in (German) relations with France as a model example". As Kaczorowska argued, "Kohl knew the power of gestures. When he (Kohl) met in September 1984 on the battlefields of Verdun with the French President Francois Mitterand, the whole world saw photos of two leaders. As they were standing over the graves of the victims, they held each other's hands in a gesture of friendship". The German Chancellor was motivated to send a similar message for the sake of Polish-German reconciliation.

On Polish side, Prime Minister Tadeusz Mazowiecki was eager to initiate a new stage in reconciliation between the two countries. Mazowiecki, like Stomma and Kisielewski, represented the Catholic intelligentsia, a group which played a pivotal role in mutual dialogue. Chancellor Kohl himself was a Catholic too. He and Premier Mazowiecki both belonged to the tradition which emphasized the importance of forgiveness, dialogue, reconciliation, and peace. There was additional element which made the Polish-German interactions at the time different: As the Soviet Leader Michail Gorbachev allowed Eastern Bloc states to act independently, both Poland and Germany could focus more on bilateral relations. It was different to the situation that occurred almost 20 years ago. Willy Brandt's visit was a part of a broader Ostpolitik, at the same time, Władysław Gomułka and other leaders of the PUWP at the time had to consider relations with the Soviet Union when contacting with Western countries.

Naturally, the new situation also brought new challenges. As the two sides were discussing the future visit of Helmut Kohl in Poland, the bishop of Opole Alfons Nossol invited the German Chancellor for attending a Catholic mass in St. Anne Mountain Sanctuary. The mass was offered to local German minority and was conducted in German language. Initially, the Germans agreed. As Katarzyna Kaczorowska noted, Helmut Kohl wished that "because of its symbolism, St. Anne could play a similar role to what Verdun had played in 1984. However, it turned out that it was precisely this symbolism which became the flashpoint in negotiations". Mieczysław Pszon, who was a prominent journalist of *Tygodnik Powszechny* and one of intellectuals engaged in Polish-German reconciliation, explained the controversy. For the Germans, the St. Anne was primarily a religious site. At the same time, the St. Anne was foremost a site of memory for Polish counterparts. During the Silesian Uprisings, the pro-Polish insurgents engaged in heavy combat with the German forces around the area of St. Anne Mountain. Organizing a mass in German language and inviting the German Chancellor for this event could have been interpreted as a provocation, which is why bishop Nossol proposed an alternative site for the mass—the Krzyżowa Village.

The site of the future Mass, Krzyżowa or Kreisau (in German), had a very complex history. Originally, the village included an estate owned by Field Marshall of Imperial Germany Helmut Kohl Bernhard von Moltke in the 19th century. However, as Katarzyna Kaczorowska noted, it was the history of field marshall's great grandson Helmuth James von Moltke which made Krzyżowa a place of meeting between Polish and German leaders. Helmuth James led an informal group of intellectuals which opposed Adolf Hitler and the Nazi party. Being aware of atrocities perpetrated by the Hitler's regime, von Moltke and his associates believed that World War II would eventually lead to downfall of the Third Reich. From 1942 to 1943, the Circle debated how the country should emerge after World War II.

After World War II and territorial changes, Kreisau was renamed Krzyżowa. History of von Moltke family and the Kreisau Circle was largely forgotten, but not entirely. As Monika Szurlej observed, local activists such as priest Bolesław Kałuża took an interest in local history. "In June 1989, such activists and researchers organized local symposium dedicated to Krzyżowa history. They proposed constructing a site which could serve the purpose of cultivating the memory about the anti-totalitarian resistance groups." Naturally, the Kreisau Circle became the most important element in this history. Eventually, the history of Krzyżowa reached bishop of Opole Alfons Nossol, the *Tygodnik Powszechny* journalist and intellectual Mieczysław Pszon and finally, premier Tadeusz Mazowiecki. For everyone, the Krzyżowa seemed a good choice for the occasion.

Helmut Kohl departed for Warsaw on 9th November 1989. He arrived in Polish capital with large delegation. Originally, everything went according to the plan. German Chancellor followed the steps of his predecessor Willy Brandt. He visited the Warsaw Ghetto Heroes Monument as Brandt did in 1970. However, Kohl received an unexpected information: The Berlin Wall fell. After a long debate, the West-German delegation decided to temporarily suspend the visit in Poland. Kohl promised his Polish counterparts that he would be back.

After the one-day visit in Berlin, Kohl went back to Poland. On 12th November 1989, he took part together with his Polish counterpart Tadeusz Mazowiecki in what was to be later remembered as the Reconciliation Mass (pol. Msza Pojednania, ger. Versöhnungs-Messe). The Mass was conducted by the Opole bishop Alfons Nossol, both in Polish and German languages. During the mass, the archbishop stressed the importance of peace and reconciliation. As the mass went on, the host asked the participants for the sign of peace—a traditional element within the Chrisitian mass. Kohl and Mazowiecki approached each other and embraced one another.

Alfons Nossol who lead the Reconciliation Mass recalled later its significance when interviewed by the local press *Gość Świdnicki*. "Its (the Reconciliation Mass) goal was to give a new beginning for building a friendship between our two nations." When commenting on the event, the bishop (and since 1999, the archbishop) reflected on the notion of peace. For him, "Peace today cannot be won ... It can only be made. After all, only at the cemetery peace can be won. It can only be done through truth and love. And by doing it, you cannot focus only on paving the way to justice, because the true soul of peace always remains in forgiveness as a special form of love."

For Polish Premier Tadeusz Mazowiecki, the Reconciliation Mass marked a new chapter for the Polish-German Reconciliation. It happened at the time when Poland underwent the political transformation. Germany, on the other hand, was about to unite into a single entity. As he recalled: "Conversations were not always easy, but they led to clarification of the disputable matters. With this Mass of Reconciliation, we continued the work begun by sending a letter from Polish bishops to the German bishops."

Both Premier Mazowiecki and archbishop Nossol emphasized two key elements of the Krzyżowa/Kreisau Reconciliation Mass. One, it was the tribute to all past reconciliation undertakings—including the bishops letter of 1965 and the Brandt's visit in 1970. But another aspect was more dedicated towards the future. Both sides predicted correctly that it was the start of the new era in Polish-German relations in new circumstances. Not so much, later on, Poland finished its political transformation: the Polish People's Republic was renamed to the Republic of Poland. The Soviet-based rule of the Polish United Workers Party was replaced with multi-parliamentary democratic rule. Meanwhile, Germany was reunited in 1990. In the same year, the German-Polish Border Treaty was signed: the Oder-Nyssse Line was finally accepted. In 1991, the Republic of Poland and the Federal Republic of Germany reached the additional agreement: the Treaty of Good Neighbourship.

More contemporary assessments are to some extent similar to opinions of those who initiated the Krzyżowa Mass. As authors of the collective work from the Krzyżowa Foundation noted: "Photos of Tadeusz Mazowiecki and Helmut Kohl who shared the peace sign with one another during the Krzyżowa Mass of 12th November 1989, became one of the most important icons of improvement of Polish-German relations in the 20th century." That being said, the Reconciliation Mass and the peace sign that leaders of Poland and Germany made received less recognition than previous gestures. Waldemar Czachur and Ryszarda Formuszewicz noted that the popular discourse gradually made Willy Brandt's *Kniefall* under the Warsaw Ghetto Heroes Monument the main icon of reconciliation. Both scholars explained the difference of popularity by pointing out the different nature of gestures. "Kneeling is a ritual gesture. Even if it draws on religious symbolism, it nevertheless is emancipated from it." Meanwhile, the peace sign in Krzyżowa was to Czachur and Formuszewicz "purely confessional": it stayed within religious symbolism of the Christian Catholic tradition.

That being said, the 1989 Reconciliation Mass proved to be an important event which maintained the continuity of the Polish-German reconciliation. Formerly, the Polish Bishops Letter to their German counterparts with other undertakings paved the way to the *Kniefall*. In a similar light we may perceive the role of Krzyżowa: together with the Border Treaty of 1990 and the Treaty of Good Neighbourship of 1991, the Reconciliation Mass influenced later developments in Warsaw.

For better understanding of later developments, we may examine additional historical context first. As both Germany and Poland entered the 1990s, both countries and nations started reassessing the period of 1945-1989. In Germany, the debate concerned the former German Democratic Republic. The reunited country had citizens who for a long time built the narrative towards the past on very different foundations. In West Germany, philosophers, politicians, historians and the society participated in the process of reckoning with the past. In the East, the Socialist Unity Party of Germany together with East German intellectuals and other social actors constructed the anti-fascist narrative. In post-reunification Germany, reintegrating the society also meant forming a narrative of united Germany towards the past. Memory of still living expellees, the anti-fascist narrative of the GDR, and the new generations influenced memory changes within the German society. Meanwhile, the Polish counterparts were reassessing memorization of the past that was constructed from 1945 to 1989. The narrative that was built during the time of the Polish People's Republic had to be rewritten, in a way that would not follow the tenants of the previous system.

Changes in the narratives were visible on specific occasions such as the commomeration of World War II. In Western Europe, the capitulation of Nazi Germany on the night of 8th/9th May 1945 was celebrated as the end of War in Europe. 8th May was labelled as the "Victory in Europe Day". Likewise, the Eastern Bloc celebrated the 9th May as the "Victory Day". Meanwhile, the anniversary was rather problematic for the Germans—how to celebrate one's defeat? As Kazimierz Wóycicki described, the first larger debate came in 1985, during the 40th Anniversary of the End of World War II. The debate focused on the issue whether or not to commemorate the anniversary. After a long public debate, which included discussions in the Bundestag and in the press, the idea of celebrating the "Remembrance Day" (ein Tag der Erinnerung) gained recognition. The idea was supported by the German President Richard von Weizsäcker at that time. For Weizsäcker and this generation of German rulers the 8th May symbolized liberation from Nazism on one hand. On the other, the date was regarded as a time of rememberance about the victims of the

Nazi Germany. 10 years later in 1995, the question was reframed: Should the Germans celebrate the 8th May as the Remembrance Day or the Victory Day? The latter was chosen, marking a shift within the narrative. This time, the new German president Roman Herzog supported the shift. As Kazimierz Wóycicki noted, Herzog and his contemporaries were more focused on the future compared to their predecessors. The change was also motivated by a generation transition—not just among the leaders of the country, but within the public opinion. The Germans who experienced their young age in the 1980s and 1990s, not only did not remember the War themselves but also felt that the period of 1933-1945 became distant a history. They were more focused on living in a new, more peaceful Europe. In short, if the 1980s were dominated by the question: "What is our national identity", then by contrast, the German public opinion of the 1990s considered another one: "Could we be the same normal country as other European ones?"

In 1994, the Polish side prepared for the 50th anniversary of the Warsaw Uprising. President Lech Wałęsa invited foreign representatives to attend the ceremony, including Presidents of Russia and Germany. The Russian President Boris Yeltsin decided not to visit Warsaw for the event. However, the invitation was accepted by the German President Roman Herzog.

It was the first time that the German head of state was to attend the anniversary of the Warsaw Uprising. In addition, even after 50 years, the memories about the insurgency were still fresh. Nevertheless, President Herzog's visit was connected with the new chapter in Polish-German reconciliation and local Warsaw peacebuilding. On 1st August, he attended official commemoration activities: one of them was paying the tribute at the Gloria Victis Monument. The main activities took place in front of the Warsaw Uprising Memorial. During his short speech, Roman Herzog delivered an important statement: "Today, I bow down before the fighters of the Warsaw Uprising as before all Polish victims of the war,(…) I ask for forgiveness for what has been done to you by Germans."

These words were very well received in Poland. This time, the German President apologized to the Poles in front of the monument specifically dedicated to the Warsaw Uprising. Sylwia Dec-Pustelnik described positive responses coming from the Polish side. The Polish president Lech Wałęsa noted that "Glory should belong to those who have courage to speak such words". Stanisław Stomma and circles of the *Tygodnik Powszechny* in general welcomed the gesture. "Stomma argued, that thanks to Herzog, the politics of reconciliation, whose merits for contemporary contacts cannot be underestimated, was recalled." Finally, the move was praised by Władysław Bartoszewski. As he argued, the visit of Roman Herzog was an inspiration for the later speech that he gave on a special occasion.

In 1995, Władysław Bartoszewski became the Polish Minister of Foreign Affairs. For the 50th anniversary of the end of World War II in Europe, the German Parliament at the time invited him to Bonn. On 28th April 1995, during a joint session of both chambers, Bartoszewski was to deliver an anniversary speech. The choice to invite him for the occasion was already symbolic. Bartoszewski took part in the civic defense of Warsaw in 1939. After being caught in 1940 by the German authorities, he was sent to Auschwitz Concentration Camp, where he remained until early 1941. Later on, he joined the resistance force of the Home Army. During the occupation, Bartoszewski took part in actions of the *Żegota*—aiding Jewish people inside the Warsaw Ghetto. Finally, he became a soldier during the Warsaw Uprising. For his service, Bartoszewski received a praise from the Home Army Warsaw District Commandant Antoni Chruściel "Monter". After being imprisoned during the time of Stalinism, Bartoszewski visited Israel, Austria, and West Germany in the 1960s. In Israel, he was received by the Yad Vashem Institute in 1963 and declared Righteous Among Nations in 1966. In Austria and Germany, he contacted politicians and intellectuals who were also interested in reconciliation as well as he stayed in touch with Polish emigration after World War II (including members of the London government). Consequently in the 1970s and 1980s, he was frequently invited to deliver lectures and speeches concerning topics of

World War II and the Jewish genocide.

Thus Bartoszewski visited in Bundestag not simply as the Polish Foreign Affairs Minister. He also came to Bonn as the former soldier of the Home Army, the Żegota member as well as the Holocaust Survivor. In his speech [Fig.3-8], he shared personal perspective with the German counterparts:

> *The Warsaw Uprising of 1944 is perpetuated in the Polish collective memory not only as an armed confrontation, but as an act of conscious barbarism: the destruction of the population of the civilian capital of Poland and the planned turning of the whole city into ruin—in the execution of Hitler's order.*

Bartoszewski emphasized the experience of Warsaw. Tragic episodes were not just a tragedy of a particular city, but also meaningful to the entire Polish nation. Despite that, Bartoszewski did not draw one-sided picture. As he stated, World War II became a catastrophe for many innocent Germans as well—especially the German expellees who, "affected by the effects of the war, have lost their homeland". Moreover, Bartoszewski expressed optimism over achievements of the reconciliation— also regarding these which were made in Warsaw. "The words of the German President Roman Herzog, spoken to the Polish nation during these celebrations in Warsaw on August 1st, 1994, were bold and sincere. Many Poles perceived them as the true, long-awaited response of the highest German representative to the message of the Polish bishops of 1965." He also recalled the significance of the Krzyżowa Mass as well as Polish-German agreements conducted in the early 1990s.

Fig.3-8 Władysław Bartoszewski during the special session of the German Parliament. During the speech, Bartoszewski referred to Warsaw experience of World War II, as the success of the Polish-German reconciliation.

All these milestones made the reconciliation possible and it was not just a matter of two countries' relations. As Bartoszewski emphasized, the Polish-German reconciliation was important for a broader European integration. The expansion of the European Union on Central Europe was possible partly because the Polish-German reconciliation was so successful—the integration would be way more difficult without it. As Bartoszewski stated: "Cooperation between the two countries united in Europe today is one of the essential objectives and justifications for bilateral relations. It gives them meaning and provides a lot of motivation."

Speeches of Roman Herzog and Władysław Bartoszewski tended to be overlooked in histories of the Polish-German reconciliation. As Sylwia Dec-Pustelnik noted, they were "not remembered in the Polish collective memory as clearly as previously mentioned initatives for the Polish-German reconciliation". That being said, "both countries made another step on a path for the better understanding during this uneasy process of negotiating the memory between the neighbors". Two speeches were also important for other reasons. They honored Warsaw: once again, Poland's capital played its role in the Polish-German dialogue, in the peace and reconciliation process. Furthermore, the two speeches were not simply directed at commemorating the past. During the same speech in Bonn, Władysław Bartoszewski reflected that "memory and historical reflection must accompany our relations. However, they should not be the main motivation for them, but they should pave the way for contemporary and forward-looking motivations". In other words, the two sides should not engage in a dialogue for the sake of honoring the past. Rather, negotiating common understanding of the past serves its role for making the present and the future. And precisely this undertaking approaches the idea of peacebuilding: using different ways of cooperation for the sake of securing peaceful future.

National reconciliation was not a matter only belonging to grand politics. The period from the 1980s to the 2000s also saw the rise of institutions and foundations dedicated to national reconciliation and the promotion of the broader peace message. Based on activities of the democratic opposition and the

Reconciliation Mass attended by Mazowiecki, the Krzyżowa Foundation was established. As we may read out from the website of the Foundation, it is "actively engaged in activities related to the peaceful co-existence of nations, social groups, and individuals. We consider bringing young people together particularly important. The purpose is to develop a spirit of responsibility and openness to others. The Foundation supports both understanding between the people and the development of European civic society". Later on, the Foundation "Polish-German Reconciliation" was founded in 1991. Based on the agreement between the two governments of Poland and Germany, the Foundation goals include commemorating history of World War II, with the special emphasis on war crimes committed by the Nazi Germany towards the Polish victims. The website (www.fpnp.pl) of the organization also lists initiating activities which promote "reconciliation and understanding between the nations, especially between the Poles and the Germans."

When it comes to promoting Polish-German reconciliation and understanding, one could also mention the Copernicus Group (Grupa Kopernika/Kopernikus Gruppe). Proposed in the year 2000 by Dieter Bingen and Kazimierz Woycicki, the group adopted a format of a think-tank which focuses mostly on contemporary Polish-German relations. People such as Klaus Bachmann, Klaus Ziemer, Basil Kerski, Adam Krzemiński, Krzysztof Ruchniewicz and many others took part in the proceedings of the group. Since 2019, the group has been led by Waldemar Czachur from the Krzyżowa Foundation and by Peter Oliver Loew from the German-Polish Institute (Deutsches-Polen Institut) in Darmstadt. Last, but not least, Warsaw possesses its own United Nations Information Committee. The Committee's role is to inform locally about the UN agenda, and to cooperate with third party institutions. Some of the projects are or are related to the peace activities.

Cherishing Peace and Reconciliation despite the Challenges

The downfall of the Eastern Bloc in 1989 and the reunification of Germany brought new perspectives for the two countries. The debate over East Germany made it possible to bring up once again the category of Germans as the victims: memories of the Stasi and the Berlin Wall were very much alive. At the same time, what was to go back was the problem of commemorating the German expellees after World War II, who thought of themselves as the victims of the War.

In 1999, the German Bundestag agreed to build the Holocaust Memorial in Berlin. The Memorial was finished in 2004 and inaugurated on 10th May 2005, 60 years after the end of World War II. Naturally, considering the circumstances, the former expellees could have thought that it was their turn that their story should be remembered. The period after the 1990s was important for Poland as well. The country still suffered the delay in changes of shifting the narrative. At the time of the Polish People's Republic, many insurgents were excluded from the narrative building. After the 1980s and 1990s, their participation in the narrative building process increased.

As two countries were redefining their national narratives, the undertakings of Erika Steinbach provoked a new debate on history. Steinbach, a daughter of a Wehrmacht soldier, had her family origins in Lower Silesia, which before the War was part of Germany and after 1945 became part of Poland. As the CDU member and a representative of the Bundestag, she voted against the Polish-German border treaty of 1990. In 1994, she was elected as the president of the German Federation of Expellees. In the year 2000, Steinbach proposed the new project: Center Against Expulsions (German: Zentrum gegen Vertreibungen, ZgV). The main idea behind the Center was to commemorate German expellees. However, since its beginning, the project faced sharp criticism on many grounds. On a more specific level, the project possessed methodological flaws, one of the examples of the definition of potential expellees. Some of the Germans who moved from contemporary Polish Western territories were not forcibly expelled, but evacuated by the German Wehrmacht or fled by their means.

But there were more fundamental objections towards the project, which made the line between the perpetrators and the victims more blurry. Former perpetrators (for instance, Nazi party members, soldiers of the Wehrmacht, or the SS functionaries) could also present themselves as the victims. On a more general level, there were concerns that the Center might have been used as a tool for moral relativism, the notion that the Germans would be perceived as the victims. As Kazimierz Wóycicki observed: "The debate over German's own victims of the war raises suspicion in Poland that other victims, especially Polish ones, are being forgotten." Because of such controversies, the project received much attention in Poland. In 2003, the mayor of Warsaw and later president Lech Kaczyński criticized Steinbach for worsening Polish-German relations. One year later, at Kaczyński's own suggestion, the Warsaw City Council summarized the material loss of Warsaw caused by the destruction during World War II. Steinbach herself resigned in 2014 as the president of the German Federation of Expellees.

Naturally, despite the controversies, the reconciliation between Poland and Germany continued. In 2000, the new German Chancellor Gerhard Schröder visited Poland, during which he also commemorated his predecessor Willy Brandt. A monument dedicated to the *Kniefall* was erected in the same year [Fig.3-9]. Delegations of German politicians appeared not only during round anniversaries of Warsaw Ghetto Uprising, Warsaw Uprising—the event of national memory, but also during anniversaries of the event of reconciliation—a notable example being the Krzyżowa (2009 and 2014). In 2014, during the 70th anniversary of the Warsaw Uprising, a major exhibition was hosted in Berlin to help German visitors to understand one of the most important events in contemporary Polish history.

Fig.3-9 Willy Brandt memorial plate. The plate, which commemorates the 30th anniversary of the Kniefall, stands in the vicinity of the Warsaw Ghetto Heroes Monument.

Fig.3-10 Prof. Liu Cheng (center right) and Prof. Egon Spiegel (right) during the visit in Warsaw, Summer 2018. Both scholars were received by the director of Museum of History of Poland Robert Kostro (center left) and Dr. Kazimierz Wóycicki (left).

The reconciliation between Poland and Germany was a major event in both countries' history, but for world history in general. Prof. Liu Cheng [Fig.3-10] stressed in his monograph *Peace Studies* (《和平学》) that reconciliation requires justice, forgiveness, truth, and peace. All these elements appeared in the Polish-German case: The justice was delivered to the victims by reparations, war crime trials, and by general admission of guilt of former perpetrators. Forgiveness was shown on both sides. Also, in the long run, both countries worked together in seeking truth. This was done by common history research, the establishment of institutions and foundations which reexamined the past. When the peaceful environment was prepared, both sides entered the dialogue.

The process continues indeed, as newer generations have different ideas on the past. However, it is difficult to talk about new ideas when they still have not fully developed. Therefore, I would like to place the "ending date" for this book on the year 2014—70th anniversary of the Warsaw Uprising. Still, before ending this part, I would like to draw attention to some issues which might be important for the later reconciliation process, where Warsaw will continue to play its role as the major site of memory.

After 2014, the majority of people born in the 1990s entered their adulthood. As time lapses, events that happened more than 70 years ago will appear more and more distant, at the same time, the last witnesses of the War will slowly disappear. How will this tendency influence the dialogue between this generation? How did the past of grandparents (and nowadays, mostly grand grandparents) affect the young Germans? For the time distance, we could assume that the generation will be less likely to feel the burden of history. At the same time, as the victimhood of the War generation becomes in a way mythological towards younger Polish generations, would the question of reconciliation be still relevant?

In this book, I mostly focused on the peace and reconciliation process in Warsaw. Here, I focused mostly on the Polish-German dialogue. However, the role of the history of the Jewish community in Warsaw from the peace research dimension should be studied as well. For the sake of clarity of the argument presented in this book, the subject of the Jewish community was limited to two main points: its destruction in Warsaw during the War and its role in the Polish-German dialogue (Brandt's symbol being a notable example). Naturally, the subject is wider, including many hotly debated topics: What was the relationship between the Polish and Jews during the War? And how later events shaped Polish-German-Jewish relations?

Going back to the Polish-German dimension,

how the past that occurred in Warsaw continues shaping contemporary Polish-German relations after 2014 remains an open question. Challenges remain, for instance, will the two sides maintain the legacy of all past milestones? We could observe that despite challenges in Polish-German relations, both countries cherished past achievements and made new gestures. In August 2019, apologies were delivered by the German Chief of Foreign Affairs Heiko Mass during the 75th anniversary of Warsaw Uprising. In September the same year, the German President Frank Walter-Steinmeier expressed apologies to the Polish side during the 80th anniversary of the outbreak of World War II.

Jerzy Wiatr in his work *The Miracle of The Reconciliation* commented that "those who emphasize difficulties and setbacks in Polish-German relations—and there are quite a few of them—tend to overlook the magnitude of change that has taken place in relations between these two nations". While agreeing with his point, we may consider that the peace and reconciliation process that occurred in Warsaw is a matter of the two nations. That being said, since we were discussing Warsaw history in a more worldwide dimension, we may also consider the importance of Polish-German reconciliation and the Warsaw experience to the broader, global audience. In a globalized world, people from other countries might be interested in the Warsaw peacebuilding and the Polish-German dialogue. This brings the question: how to tell that story to others? How does Warsaw engage in broader peace culture today?

Suggestions of past scholars can be taken into account, that the experience of the Polish-German dialogue could provide an inspiration for the topic of national reconciliation. These experiences could also be used in peace education and in building broader peace culture.

Regarding Warsaw, we saw that the city maintains its title of the Peace Messenger City, many of its sites within the city are connected with the Polish-German reconciliation. But apart from that, on a more everyday level, some sites of memory in Warsaw integrate elements of peace culture. An initiative which was proposed by the Warsaw Rising Museum could be one of such examples. The Pavilion, which is called in Polish "Pokój na Lato" [Fig.3-11], was designed in a manner to resemble summer resorts in Warsaw outskirts. As the Warsaw Rising Museum representatives stated, the place was designed to host workshops, concerts, lectures dedicated to the history of Warsaw, film sessions, retro dance parties, and others. "The location of the Pavilion is not accidental. Being founded next to Warsaw Uprising, 'Pokój na Lato' completes the narrative of the museum. It is a space for dialogue, meetings, and relaxation. Everyone for whom Warsaw is home will have his room in Wola (district)." The name of the Pavilion is itself playing with words. It could be translated to "Summer Room" as well as the "Summer Peace." Thus, in a way, the peace culture is promoted. The inclusion of the peace dove strengthens the message.

Fig.3-11 Warsaw Rising Museum Pavilion called Pokój na Lato. The Pavilion "Pokój na Lato" opened in the year 2015.

The organizers stressed that the Summer Peace/Summer Room Pavilion provided a more leisure program which contrasted with the "serious anniversary events." This "is underlined by the name itself—next to martyrdom, we have a temporary room". Where there is a space for those who should be remembered forever, there is also a space for temporary relax. The contrast is stressed with the existence of the footbridge [Fig.3-12] "that crosses two walls—the surrounding Museum area and the Memorial Wall, on which the names of the fallen are engraved".

Such a construction is an important one. It shows that while remembering history, we may still cherish peace, in a way that it will be respectful towards the past, but also in a way that enables us to proceed with the future. The idea of organizers was to create a green space linked with the Warsaw Rising Museum which would offer educational-cultural activities to the inhabitants. After visiting the "sacred sphere" of the Warsaw Rising Museum, the visitors could turn for a relaxing program, offering them lectures on the history of Warsaw, musicals, art performances. Used symbols [Fig.3-13] and the subtle name-game made by organizers—"Summer Peace" and "Summer Room"—also stresses that people may find here peace.

Warsaw Peace and Reconciliation Process is strongly linked with the achievements of the Polish-German dialogue and the direct peacebuilding in Poland's capital after the War. It could also mean promoting peace culture in an official way: through state-to-state anniversaries and initiatives of well established organizations. That being said, it could also be about simpler things: cherishing everyday peaceful life.

Fig.3-12 The footbridge separating two walls: one surrounding the Museum, the other being the Memorial Wall.

Fig.3-13 The peace dove symbol featured in the "Summer Peace" or "Summer Room" (Pokój na lato). The site was thought to be a complimentary space to the Warsaw Rising Museum. If the main role of the Museum is to discuss the Warsaw Uprising and wartime Warsaw, the "Summer Peace" organizes activities dedicated to Warsaw in the past—at the time of peace.

Reconciliation is a process and never ends. Reconciliation is an attitude toward others. Either it is open and benevolent about others, or not. Reconciliation is not the process of forgetting, but rather an attitude to the other man. For generations that survived the War, this is certainly much harder to obtain than for the next generations. But I see that, after all, this process continues.

— Tadeusz Mazowiecki, former Polish Prime Minister

This book focused primarily on the story of Warsaw. Its past becomes part of national pride, but also a symbol of the nation's foremost disaster—World War II. Once proud Poland's capital emerged after the conflict was completely devastated. What was to be rebuilt were not just buildings, but also people's memories. Puzzles of memories await to be pinched together into one coherent picture—also to reconcile with the past and to build peace. Warsaw's experience, apart from its peacebuilding aspect, was also a part of broader Polish-German reconciliation. Regarding the Polish-German reconciliation, once I heard an opinion from a local friend: "The Germans were so nice to the Poles—their chancellor apologized for the War." However, reconciliation never happens solely on the knowledge about what happened. It always happens with the reference to what the two sides remember from the past. In this sense, reconciliation is a dialogue.

Poles and Germans together did a lot of work for this dialogue. By pinching together puzzles of memory, in Warsaw and elsewhere, they eventually succeeded in reconciliation. And they still engage in dialogue since it is never a finished process. For now, we may reconsider why this reconciliation was successful to use its fruits for more practical deeds—to educate future generations on peace and reconciliation. We may consider how Warsaw experience is presented and promoted to the international audience—also for the sake of promoting peace culture.

To paraphrase earlier paraphrasing of Stanisław Stomma, this endeavor is worthy of its effort—not just for Warsaw people, not just for the Poles and the Germans, but for the broader global community.

Main Bibliography

1. Anderson, Benedict, Imagined Communities: Reflections on the Origin and Spread of Nationalism, Revised ed. Edition, London, New York: Verso, 2016.

2. Barcz, Jan, Ruchniewicz Krzysztof, Akt Dobrosąsiedzki, 30 lat Traktatu Polsko-Niemieckiego o Dobrym Sąsiedztwie i Przyjaznej Współpracy, Wrocław, Warszawa: Dom Wydawniczy Elipsa, 2021.

3. Bingen, Dieter, Wóycicki Kazimierz, Grupa Kopernika, Komunikaty i raporty z posiedzeń 2000-2012, we współpracy z Krzysztofem Ruchniewiczem, Wrocław: Oficyna Wydawnicza Atut, 2013.

4. Boutros-Ghali, Boutros, An Agenda for Peace: Preventive Diplomacy, Peacemaking and Peace-keeping: Report of the Secretary-General Pursuant to the Statement Adopted by the Summit Meeting of the Security Council on 31 January, 1992.

5. Czachur, Waldemar, Franke Annemarie, Krzyżowa jako miejsce dialogu polsko-niemieckiego. Szanse na Europejską Narrację, Msza Pojednania w Krzyżowej Fundacja Krzyżowa dla Porozumienia Europejskiego, 2013.

6. Czupryński, Andrzej, Huzarski Michał, Wojna i pokój przedmiotem badań polemologiczno-irenologicznych, Warszawa: Akademia Obrony Narodowej, 2012.

7. Collective Work, Radio Free Europe Research, Situation Report, Poland, 5.02.1986.

8. Davies, Norman, Rising '44: The Battle for Warsaw, New York: Macmillan, 2003.

9. Dec-Pustelnik, Sylwia, Historia a pamięć: Pojednanie Polsko-Niemieckie w Dyskursie Medialnym, Wrocław: Wydawnictwo Atut, 2019.

10. Drozdowski, Marian Marek, Zahorski Andrzej, Historia Warszawy, Warszawa: Wydawnictwo Jeden Świat, 2004.

11. Ehrlich, L., Pisma wybrane Pawła Włodkowica, t. 1, Warszawa, 1968.

12. Frieberg, Annika Elisabet, Peace at All Costs: Catholic Intellectuals, Journalists, and Media in Postwar Polish-German Reconciliation, New York: Berghahn, 2019.

13. Głodni, Warszawy otwieramy, "Pokój na lato"—letni pawilon rekreacyjno-kulturalny, [w:]https://www.1944.pl/artykul/glodni-warszawy-otwieramy-pokoj-na-lato,4467.html, stan na 22.08.2020.

14. Głogowski, Mirosław, Kamiński Leszek, Collective work, Congress of Intellectuals for a Peaceful Future of the World, Warsaw: Interpress, 1988.

15. Gość Świdnicki. nr. 47/293, 22 listopada, 2009.

16. Hobsbawm, Eric, The Invention of Tradition, Cambridge: Cambridge University Press, 1983.

17. "International Year of Peace", United Nations resolution, November 16, 1992.

18. Janaszek, Seydlitz, Historia zapomnianego cmentarza, Komitet ds. Cmentarza Powstańców Warszawy przy Światowym Związku Żołnierzy AK, Warszawa: Stowarzyszenie Pamięci Powstania Warszawskiego, 2017.

19. Kucharski, Wojciech, Listy Milenijne, Wrocław: Ośrodek "Pamięć i Przyszłość", 2020.

20. Liu, Cheng, Egon Spiegel, Peacebuilding in a Globalized World. An Illustrated Introduction to Peace Studies, Beijing: People's Publishing House, 2015.

21. Murphy, Dean E., Germany Asks for Poland's Forgiveness : Europe: Apology issued on the 50th Anniversary of the Warsaw Uprising. Los Angeles Times, 2 August 1994.

22. Napiórkowski, Marcin, Powstanie umarłych. Historia pamięci 1944-2014, Warszawa: Wydawnictwo Krytyki Politycznej, 2014.

23. "Pokój na lato"—pawilon rekreacyjno-kulturalny, [w:] https://www.1944.pl/artykul/pokoj-na-lato-pawilon-rekreacyjno-kulturaln,4330.html, stan na 22.08.2020.

24. Pokój na lato, [w:], https://h2architekci.com/portfolio/pokoj-na-lato/, stan na 22.08.2020.

25. Praca, Zbiorowa, Kongres Pokoju (Warszawa, 16-22.XI. 1950), Warszawa: Książka i Wiedza, 1950.

26. Praca, Zbiorowa, Walczymy o pokój na świecie, Warszawa: Wydawnictwo Głównego Komitetu Kultury Fizycznej, 1951.

27. Sawicki, Jacek Zygmunt, Bitwa o prawdę. Historia Zmagań o Pamięć Powstania Warszawskiego 1944-1989, Wydawnictwo DiG, Warszawa, 2005.

28. Skonieczny, Tomasz, Msza Pojednania w Krzyżowej, Wrocław: Fundacja Krzyżowa dla Porozumienia Europejskiego, 2019.

29. Stomma, Stanisław, Czy Fatalizm wrogości? Refleksje o stosunkach polsko-niemieckich 1871-1933, Wrocław, 2005.

30. Stojanović, Dušan, "15 Years of the IAPMC (1986-2001)" Brochure, Koroška tiskarna Slovenj Gradec: International Association of Peace Messenger Cities & Slovenj Gradec, 2001.

31. Sztompke, Ewa, Nietuzinkowe historie pomników Warszawy. Opowieści warszawskiej przewodniczki, Warszawa: Wydawnictwo Weda, 2019.

32. The Holy See, Apostolic Journey to Poland Holy Mass Homily of his Holiness John Paul II, Victory Square, Warsaw, 2 June 1979.

33. Webel, Charles, Johan Galtung, Handbook of Peace and Conflict Studies, London: Routledge, 2007.

34. Wiatr, Jerzy, Polish-German Relations: The Miracle of Reconciliation, Leverkusen: Barbara Budrich Publishers, 2014.

35. Woźniczka, Zygmunt, Wrocławski Kongres Intelektualistów w Obronie Pokoju, Kwartalnik Historyczny R. 94 nr 2 (1987), s. 131-157.

36. Wóycicki, Kazimierz, Niemiecka pamięć. Rozrachunek z przeszłością NRD i przemiany niemieckiej świadomości historycznej, Warszawa, 2011.

37. Wóycicki, Kazimierz, Niemiecki rachunek sumienia : Niemcy wobec przeszłości 1933-1945, Wrocław: ATUT- Wrocławskie Wydaw. 2004.

38. Zamoyski, Adam, Poland: A History, New York: Hippocrene Books, 2012.

39. 刘成:《和平学》, 南京 : 南京出版社, 2006 年。

Afterword

This book is a part of a series entitled the *International Cities of Peace*. As Prof. Liu Cheng mentioned in his Preface, Warsaw was included in the series: Nanjing, Dresden, Hiroshima and Coventry were also chosen for this project and received their own separate publications.

Throughout the project, I perceived my role as someone who wished that could synthesize knowledge of different study fields: Peace Studies and Peace Research, History of Warsaw and Poland, Memory and Narrative Studies, the Polish-German Reconciliation analysis. All these different elements of the puzzle combined together could, I believe, present a clear picture: Warsaw as the Peace City, its tragic past and subsequent rememberance, the role of the city in shaping peace and reconciliation: in Polish-German dialogue and beyond it.

I would like to first thank Prof. Liu Cheng of Nanjing University for the main guidance and proposed I write this book. Prof. Liu is the leading scholar on peace studies in China and the Holder of the UNESCO Chair on Peace Studies. When we started the book project more than four years ago, I felt intrigued by his academic approach and sympathy towards peace studies idea. His idea to make a book series on wartime cities and the postwar peace and reconciliation process is an endeavor worthy of being supported.

Prof. Liu was my mentor for peace studies, Dr. Kazimierz Wóycicki from University of Warsaw was my guide through the Warsaw collective memory and the Polish-German reconciliation. Dr. Wóycicki has been leading the Eastern Academy of the Eastern House (Akademia Wschód. Dom Wschodni) which promotes dialogue on history and peaceful coexistence between the nations of Central Europe. Apart from scholarly guidance, Dr. Wóycicki provided valuable suggestions for the book structure and its visual materials. In addition, I owe him some of the photos which appear in this publication.

Both Prof. Liu and Dr. Wóycicki made major contributions to this publication. That being said, there were also other scholars whose work I found very valuable during the writing process. I would like to thank Prof. Egon Spiegel from the University of Vechta and Dr. Elly Hallowell, both being respected scholars in peace studies.

But the project did not just involve full-time academics, but also fellow students and young scholars. For their support during the writing process and broader academic cooperation, I would like to thank Dr. Bai Shuang, Luo Qingyun, Lu Deting, Wang Xiaoyang, all of them being involved in World Peace Cities project as authors. Then, I would like to thank Nanjing Normal University Press representatives for publishing this work, including Xu Lei, Zheng Haiyan, Wang Yaqiong, and Liu Shuangshuang. I would also like to thank Prof. Zhang Tong. Based on this English edition and its materials, Dr. Zhang Tong prepared the Chinese version. The two editions differ in content due to different ideas proposed by the authors. The readers are welcomed to study both editions of the publication.

Last but not least, many thanks to my friends in Nanjing and Warsaw, my girlfriend Lee Xiao Shiang, and my family members. Their good words encouraged me to carry on with my work. Eventually, all earlier-mentioned efforts finally resulted in this monograph.

Rzeszów, 15.04.2022
Kuala Lumpur, 05.08.2022

For Photo Credits Please Refer to